WHY DEMOCRACY NEEDS PUBLIC GOODS

WHY DEMOCRACY NEEDS PUBLIC GOODS

Angela Kallhoff

LEXINGTON BOOKS

A division of
ROWMAN & LITTLEFIELD PUBLISHERS, INC.
Lanham • Boulder • New York • Toronto • Plymouth, UK

Published by Lexington Books
A division of Rowman & Littlefield Publishers, Inc.
A wholly owned subsidiary of The Rowman & Littlefield Publishing Group, Inc.
4501 Forbes Boulevard, Suite 200, Lanham, Maryland 20706
www.lexingtonbooks.com

Estover Road, Plymouth PL6 7PY, United Kingdom

British Library Cataloguing in Publication Information Available

Library of Congress Cataloging-in-Publication Data

Kallhoff, Angela.
Why democracy needs public goods / Angela Kallhoff.
p. cm.
Includes bibliographical references and index.
ISBN 978-0-7391-5100-6 (cloth : alk. paper)
ISBN 978-0-7391-6800-4 (ebook)
1. Public goods. I. Title.
HB846.5.K35 2011
330.1'7—dc22

2011012818

∞™ The paper used in this publication meets the minimum requirements of American National Standard for Information Sciences—Permanence of Paper for Printed Library Materials, ANSI/NISO Z39.48-1992.

Printed in the United States of America

CONTENTS

ACKNOWLEDGMENTS

This book is the result of research on public goods at the University of Chicago. I would especially like to thank the colleagues at the University of Chicago, who welcomed the project, supported me in developing my ideas, and were always ready to discuss my approach. I am particularly indebted to Clark W. Gilpin, Martha C. Nussbaum, Winnifred Fallers Sullivan, and the members of the Martin E. Marty Research Seminar of 2004–2005.

Parts of chapter 7 were published in *Criterion* Vol. 44, Spring 2005, A Publication of the University of Chicago Divinity School.

I also wish to thank Jana Wilson of Lexington Books. Throughout the publication process, it was a great pleasure to work with her. A special thanks goes to Franziska Quabeck who corrected the manuscript and gave me advice when my language skills did not suffice to express my insights sharply.

The entire project was supported by a Feodor Lynen grant from the Alexander von Humboldt Foundation, Germany. I also received a grant as a senior research fellow from the Martin E. Marty Center at the University of Chicago. I wish to express my gratitude for the generous support from these institutions, both in terms of professional and personal care.

My deepest appreciation goes to my husband Thomas and my son Timon. Thomas was always ready to provide help and support for the project was whatever was needed.

1

INTRODUCING PUBLIC GOODS

Public goods differ from private goods. They are not the property of individuals. Instead, they are upheld by communities. Moreover, people can enjoy public goods together, sometimes even without competing with each other over the benefits. Examples of public goods are public parks and public schools, infrastructure and some environmental goods such as water and sunshine. The peculiarities of public goods have not remained unnoticed. Yet, theories on public goods have primarily been developed in the fields of public finance and in theories on collective choice, which generally focus on bad side effects of public goods regimes.

In this study, I wish to present a theoretical alternative to those approaches. The general thesis is that public goods are useful in supporting democracy. The approach relies on a thorough examination of the particular characteristics of public goods and begins with findings about their specific structure. These characteristics have been described as such: As for potential beneficiaries of public goods, these items are non-excludable and they do not evoke rivalry. Even though these characteristics have been revised, they are still useful as a starting point to explain the special quality of public goods. The approach that will be presented in this study then discusses public goods in the context of contemporary political philosophy.

Even though public goods have not been central to debates in that field of research, political philosophy is the suitable frame for two reasons. *First*, it explores societies not with an empirical interest; instead, political philosophers work within the normative assumption that democratic societies need certain preconditions to flourish. From that perspective, the interest in public goods should not simply be described as the desire of consumers to get support for leading a good life. Instead, political philosophers are interested in how private and public interests can be balanced against each other. Correspondingly, the central claim is not that public goods fulfill the interests of citizens. Instead, a political philosophy of public goods defends the stronger claim that these items strengthen those societal structures which are an integral part of democracies. More precisely, I shall defend the claims that public goods support social justice and the sense of effective equality among citizens and—among other effects—thereby also provide a necessary background for the public forum.

The *second* reason for choosing political philosophy as a frame for this study is the ongoing endeavor to think about means that make democracy a better place to live in. In that respect, public goods theory can contribute to a larger debate. Today, there is a deep concern about the future of our Western democracies, since there are many troublesome developments: The gaps between rich and poor increase; political society loses its common ground and something like a broad center—instead many people are either politically uninterested or driven to extreme positions; the European welfare state is at risk. Simultaneously, governments gain new and even unprecedented roles. In this situation, the commitment of governments either to invest in public goods or to restrict spending on public goods is a forceful instrument to answer to some of the challenges that have been listed.

In this study, I will not argue that public goods are a panacea for the ailments of Western societies. I shall rather explore arguments that underpin the thesis, that in some important respects, public goods can provide the common focus of citizens. And I shall argue that from the perspective of political philosophy those reasons can be made explicit.

This first chapter serves as an introduction to the central themes of this study. It is organized in four sections. I shall *first* introduce a description of public goods that goes back to studies in public finance in the 20th century. Interestingly, this description is open to two different interpretations. I shall explain them in turn and present my way of coping with what might be called the "double face" of public goods. *Secondly*, I shall introduce the arguments in favor of public goods that are at the heart of this study. They have been developed within the field of political theory and comprise arguments from theories of justice, theories on the public, and theories of democracy. *Third*, I will need to make some comments on the list of diverse items that can all be called public goods. Since each theory on public goods needs to make clear how it is possible to cope with the rich variety of different items that all fit the description, I shall give a list of headlines that serve as a first orientation. I shall also give a brief comment on my understanding of democracy. *Fourth*, it contains a prospect of the chapters of this book.

TWO PERSPECTIVES ON PUBLIC GOODS

In the 20th century, economists were aware of the peculiarities of public goods. In particular, they compared public goods to private goods and succeeded in developing a precise and until today remarkable definition. Paul Samuelson characterizes public goods as goods "which all enjoy in common in the sense that each individual's consumption of such a good leads to no substraction from any other individual's consumption of that good."[1] In Samuelson's view, non-rivalry in consumption is the distinctive feature of public goods. Richard A. Musgrave, on the other hand, emphasizes non-excludability as a characteristic property of public goods. He notes that "there are some situations where excludability is impossible (defence) and others where it is available at little or no cost (ice cream or use of bridge). In the former case, we have no choice in the matter."[2] Even though pure cases of public goods are rare, irregularities in terms of rivalry and excludability can still be considered the most characteristic features of public goods.[3]

At first glance, theories that explore the defining properties of public goods do not have a normative content. They are neutral in the sense that they do not imply a particular value commitment. But, as a matter of fact, in interpreting public goods, two completely different routes can be taken. Research on public goods is split into two different camps and this split is also reflected in the general opinion on these items. On the one hand, public goods have primarily been considered to be troublemakers. Even though most agree that the sustenance of some public goods is part of the noblest endeavors of the nation-state, many authors also agree that the range needs to be restricted for theoretical reasons. One needs to restrict the policies to some core functions of the nation-state because public goods are particularly costly and need support through tax policies and because normative ideas about the freedom and liberties of citizens.[4] On the other hand, public goods are considered an essential ingredient in democracies.

The latter view has recently been put forward by Tony Judt.[5] Whereas *Ill Fares the Land* covers a wide range of different items, one argument focuses on a development of what Judt calls "The Cult of the Private" and the loss of common goods.[6] For our purpose, two conclusions that Judt draws from the loss of public goods are important. *First*, in Judt's view, "the thick mesh of social interactions and public goods has been reduced to a minimum."[7] As a consequence, "we have begun to dismantle the fabric of the state."[8] This loss of "shared citizenship"[9] contributes to a democratic deficit that cannot easily be repaired. *Secondly*, public goods also figure as "visual representations of collective identity."[10] Buses and trains, the arts, armies, the police, public space, and public highways[11] are not only useful and necessary instruments to organize political society. Following Judt, they also symbolize that—in some cases—common interests should trump private interests.

In this study, I shall place emphasis on this second perspective on public goods. It is my aim to examine its underlying arguments. Yet, I think it would be short-sighted to neglect the first perspective on public goods. Of course, they might be costly. And of course, commitment of governments to public goods has implications that need to be seen and that need to be handled with care. My way of coping with the twofold face of public goods can best be described as an approach that strengthens the second perspective without neglecting the first. I wish to achieve this goal by reconsidering the range of arguments that have already been made in favor and against public goods and adding some more from political philosophy.

CONTEXT OF ANALYSIS

The scientific context for analyzing public goods in this study is contemporary political philosophy. Discussing public goods from this perspective includes a slight refinement of the initial definition. But—most importantly—arguments will be developed in a normative frame. The discussion starts with the question of why this special group of items, which can be given a precise description because of its peculiarities, should exist and why it should be supported. Furthermore, the definition sets public goods apart from further groups of goods that might otherwise get mixed up with them. Public goods differ from state-owned goods; property rights are not the decisive feature. Public goods also must *not* to be conflated with welfare goods. Welfare goods are goods that help overcome poverty and they are goods that are distributed along the lines of social justice. Public goods, however, are not related to these aims, but are accessible by each person simultaneously and non-discriminately.

The method I shall employ in my philosophical analysis can best be described as a *focal analysis*. It can be compared to what economists tried out with public goods about half a century ago. They imported public goods as a special group of goods into a field of economic analysis that focuses on private goods. In effect, interesting characteristics could be revealed and effects on the system were determined. Through importing public goods into contemporary political philosophy, some fundamental links between public goods and democracy will be revealed. In detail, in examining the role of public goods in a political community that subscribes to democratic values, four reasons why public goods should be sustained and cultivated become apparent.

First, I shall argue that public goods are necessary preconditions for the evolvement and preservation of the public. Instead of limiting this function to goods that particularly support public deliberation and stimulate the public forum, it is due to the non-exclusivity of this special group of goods. Furthermore, public goods provide a realm in society that strengthens mutual awareness and helps to generate a sense of shared citizenship.

Secondly, public goods respond to justified claims of social justice. Since Rawls's *A Theory of Justice* was published,[12] the debate on social justice has not come to an end. I shall contribute to that debate in reflecting on goods whose access barriers are surmountable by all citizens. This provides an interesting turn because, at first sight, public goods do not match the distributive paradigm that is prevalent in current theories on social justice. They cannot even be distributed in the strict sense. Yet, a thorough analysis reveals that public goods contribute to enhancing the conditions of social justice. Instead of primarily contributing to poverty-prevention, public goods support social inclusion.

Third, diversity in public goods supports the conditions for a reasonable pluralism in modern societies. The kind of pluralism that public goods support leads back neither to integralism nor to colorless societies that exclusively build on political institutions. Within their history, public goods have been at the center of civil society. As related to the long history of public goods, the welfare state has only recently surfaced as an important supporter. Instead of exclusively relying on state-governed public goods, it is reasonable to strengthen participation of private associations in common goods. Yet, preconditions have to be formulated so that liberal societies can cope with value commitments in the public that relate to public goods.

Fourth, public goods strengthen democracy in that they provide a necessary supplement to the guarantee of basic rights. They help citizens to identify with the political community that—through public goods—has a particular outlook.

DIVERSITY AND DEMOCRACY

Before presenting the content of this study in more detail, I need to say something about the range of items that fall under the definition of a public good. I also need to say something about my understanding of democracy. The latter is necessary in order to interpret the claim that *democracy needs public goods*.

One specific problem in dealing with public goods results from the rich diversity of items that all fall under the description of a public good. Even when the range of public goods is restricted through a precise definition—something that will be done in the next chapter—this will not significantly decrease the diversity of items that figure as public goods. For these reasons, it is helpful to give an idea of the range of objects right at the beginning. This can be done by spelling out six different headlines that refer to special groups of public goods that have been the subject of discussion.

Those headlines are: security, infrastructure, education and science, environmental goods, culture and cultural heritage, and institutions of care. In each of the areas, typical examples can be listed. *Security* comprises domestic security and outer security. As for *infrastructure*, the lighthouse, infrastructure for telecommunication, streets, and highways are typical examples. As for *education and science*, public goods are exemplified in public schools, universities, and libraries as well as in institutions of knowledge-sharing such as the media. Water, sun, and renewable energy are examples of *environmental goods*. Typical examples of *culture and cultural heritage* as public goods comprise broadcasting, the public theater, and traditional objects and instantiations of arts as well as entertainment and public events. Typical examples of *institutions of care* as public goods are hospitals that each person is allowed to enter and to profit from in an emergency and a public health care system.

This list is not meant to be exhaustive; nor does it imply that all listed items necessarily need to exemplify the structure of a public good. Instead, the listed items are candidates for public goods as discussed in this study.

Before presenting the contents of the chapter in more detail, I also need to explain the concept of democracy that figures within the argument that *democracy needs public goods*. One of the most distinguishing features of theories on democracy in the field of political philosophy is that they go beyond analyzing the institutional design of a democratic state. Even though this is part of the endeavor to explain democracy, theories in political philosophy primarily focus on the normative ideas implicit in the concept of democracy.[13] Philosophers also reason about the structures and institutions that are needed to express these values, but it is not their main interest.

This feature can be explained by turning to constitutional democracy: This is the form of democracy that we are best acquainted with in the Western world. As Walter F. Murphy argues, "constitutional democracy is a political hybrid, resting on a pair of normative political theories that are usually compatible but coexist in a state of tension and occasionally in open conflict."[14] And he goes on to say: "Constitutionalist and democratic theorists differ on many points, but they agree that government, society, and individual citizens are obliged to treat all citizens with great and equal respect. More specifically, both see each person as a carrier of rights and responsibilities."[15] In this study, I shall rely on this broad understanding of the common point of reference of theories on democracy. In my view, the core values that Murphy alludes to can also be expressed in terms of a shared bundle of political values. Among the most basic political values—as opposed to private values that citizens do not subscribe to as citizens but rather as private persons[16]—are social and political justice. Even though both concepts need interpretation, they reflect the basic rights of citizens that Murphy addresses in his interpretation of constitutional democracy.

Following John Rawls, a second set of political values relates to public reason.[17] Citizens should be free to express their opinion; they should be in a situation to contribute to a public forum. In explaining the function of public goods in democracy, I shall come closest to the theoretical background of deliberative democracy. Theories of deliberative democracy express an important insight. They say that democracy cannot be explained without also taking into account civil society and its power in forming a public.[18] In my understanding of deliberative democracy, it does not compete with liberal democracy—a strand of thought that stresses the basic rights and liberties of citizens. Deliberative democracy, instead, focuses on one aspect of democracy which is particularly important for understanding the impact of public goods on democracy.

PROSPECT

My approach to public goods is presented in seven chapters.

In chapter two, the theoretical background that will be employed throughout this book shall be outlined. I shall first go back to the classical notion of public goods that was developed by Samuelson and Musgrave. The second section then gives a definition of public goods that comes close to the original definition. But—in contrast to that approach—it contains a slightly different interpretation of "non-excludability" and of "non-rivalry." I shall discuss this notion in comparing public goods to similar groups of goods, since it is important to distinguish public goods both from welfare goods and from state-owned goods. Further refinements of my theoretical approach help narrow down the group of items that will actually count as public goods in this book. At the end of chapter two, I shall present a list of public goods that comprises the items that fit the conditions set through the definition and its refinements.

In chapter three, I shall go back to a wide spread perspective on public goods. This is the theory of public goods as it was developed in theories on public finance and from the perspective of collective action problems. Chapter 3 provides a critical stance on these theories; it also includes a critique of some of its most important implications. This chapter does not intend to present a new approach to public goods. It should rather contribute to getting a realistic view of the problems that public goods might cause in terms of inefficiency and market failures.

In chapter four, I shall argue that public goods contribute to generating the public. If they succeed in doing so, they can be called *connectivity goods*. The argument is that public goods provide conditions that help citizens to understand themselves as parts of a larger community of equal citizens. Furthermore, they provide a realm within society that helps citizens to connect with each other. This approach to public goods does not only shift the perspective, it also contributes to modifying two alternatives in the debate on the public within the camp of political philosophy. *First*, a functional approach to the public that defines it along the lines of coping with negative externalities neglects the need for goods as a focus of the public. In his theory of the public, John Dewey defends a functional approach to the evolvement of governmental structures. He says that the awareness of severe and unintended consequences of collective action significantly contributes to the evolvement of the public.[19] Reconsidering public goods helps to cope with some of the difficulties in that approach to the public. *Secondly*, Jürgen Habermas provides an influential interpretation of the public as a realm within democracy that exemplifies a particular structure. The public is built through processes of communication among free and equal citizens.[20] My argument is *not* that this interpretation needs to be corrected; on the contrary, my argument is that Habermas does not pay enough attention to the preconditions of the public forum. I shall argue that public goods provide the conditions for a public to flourish. Instead of focusing exclusively on deliberation, I place emphasis on a material basis of the public. This perspective on the public also contributes to modifying some aspects of Habermas's theory of the public forum.

In chapter five, I shall defend the claim for a distinct range of public goods as a claim for social justice. The range of goods that support a situation of social justice will be called *central public goods*. Since public goods have not been in the focus of theories on justice, I first need to explore theoretical possibilities of integrating public goods into those theories. In contrasting various theoretical perspectives on public goods, it becomes apparent that the capabilities approach of Martha C. Nussbaum provides the theoretical framework to select a range of public goods that are pivotal to issues of social justice.[21] I shall also introduce a principle of fairness that relates to the normative ideas of public goods in terms of goods that support social inclusion.

Again, introducing public goods into the debate also has an effect on the understanding of social justice. Instead of defining social justice exclusively in terms of distribution according to principles of fairness, an approach that focuses on public goods places emphasis on the concept of social inclusion. I shall also argue that this new approach to social justice contributes to overcoming some notorious dilemmas of exclusively distributive accounts, but still answers to some of the widespread ideas of social justice—namely, claims to protect the worst-off and claims to offer equal opportunities to all citizens.

In chapter six, I shall discuss how public goods regimes relate to concepts of political self-determination. Because of the impact public goods policies have on citizens, the legitimating of political decisions regarding public goods has been regarded to be central. Without authorization through the citizenry, public goods regimes tend to have despotic structures—both regarding tax policies and regulation. Yet, unanimity is hard to achieve. My main argument in chapter 6 is that this critique relies on an understanding of political self-determination that reduces it to political mechanisms of representation. I shall argue that public goods—when situated within civil society—serve a self-confident citizenry. In that case, they will be called *identification goods*.

In chapter seven, I shall turn to a critical assessment of public goods. This has primarily been debated among political philosophers from the liberal camp. Even though authors in the tradition of political liberalism provide strong arguments for governmental duties regarding collective goods, they are not necessarily inclined to favoring a broad support of a wide range of public goods. A short look back at the history of two particularly value-laden public goods, education and health care, helps understand one problem that liberals address. These goods have been provided by religious and civil bodies that subscribe to distinctive value statements. Even though the involvement of the nation-state may push public goods onto a more neutral ground, it is essential to understand that public goods cannot be regarded as neutral things. Instead of regarding this as a major problem, I shall argue that it offers a particular chance when three dimensions of value commitments are thoroughly distinguished. The three value dimensions which have to be kept apart are: the values which participants in public goods may import into the sphere of a public good; the values which the providers and supporters of public goods might subscribe to; and the values which are inherent in a particular good, say health care or education. I shall argue that a separation of these spheres of values contributes to rethinking the ideas of tolerance and pluralism as related to public goods regimes.

In chapter eight, a group of influential counterarguments against public goods will be discussed. Public goods have primarily been handled with caution because of the undesirable side effect in terms of political regulation and in terms of intervention as a practice that has distorting effects on the economy. In political philosophy, a group of philosophers who are called libertarians have made this claim explicit. Yet, a closer look at these theories shows that several aspects that need to be distinguished have been mixed up. In particular, normative arguments need to be distinguished from empirical ones. A differentiation of various levels of argumentation and a thorough examination of the claims help to dismantle some of those libertarian arguments. In particular, a reassessment of the value of public goods also needs to include a reassessment of capacities of markets as compared to the capacities of political institutions.

A conclusion at the end of the book serves to bind the various strands of arguments together. It also includes two recommendations for shaping public goods regimes in order to support the effects that will be discussed here.

NOTES

1. Paul A. Samuelson, "The Pure Theory of Public Expenditure," in *The Theory of Market Failure: A Critical Examination*, ed. by Tyler Cowen (Fairfax, VA: George Mason University Press, 1988), 29.

2. Richard A. Musgrave, "Provision for Social Goods," in *Public Economics: An Analysis of Public Production and Consumption and Their Relations to the Private Sectors*, ed. by J. Margolis and H. Guitton (London: Macmillan; New York: St. Martin's Press, 1969), 128.

3. Inge Kaul, Isabelle Grunberg, and Marc Stern "Defining Global Public Goods," in *Global Public Goods: International Cooperation in the 21st Century*, ed. by Inge Kaul, Isabelle Grunberg, and Marc Stern (New York and Oxford: Oxford University Press, 1999), 3–4.

4. I shall discuss these arguments in length in chapter 8.

5. Tony Judt, *Ill Fares the Land* (New York: Penguin Press, 2010).

6. Judt, *Ill Fares*, 106–119.

7. Judt, *Ill Fares*, 118.

8. Judt, *Ill Fares*, 119.

9. Judt, *Ill Fares*, 121.

10. Judt, *Ill Fares*, 123.

11. These are some of the examples that Judt discusses in *Ill Fares*, 123–129.

12. John Rawls, *A Theory of Justice* (Cambridge, MA: Harvard University Press, 1971).

13. For an overview on theories of democracy in the tradition of political philosophy *see* David Held, *Models of Democracy* (2nd ed., Stanford, CA: Stanford University Press 1996).

14. Walter F. Murphy, *Constitutional Democracy: Creating and Maintaining a Just Political Order* (Baltimore: Johns Hopkins University Press, 2007), 345.

15. Murphy, *Constitutional Democracy*, 345–346.

16. For this distinction *see* John Rawls, *Political Liberalism* (New York: Columbia University Press, 1996), 30–31.

17. Rawls, *Political Liberalism*, 139.

18. In discussing the impact of public goods on "the public" in chapter 4, the theoretical background of deliberative democracy will be discussed in more detail.

19. John Dewey, *The Public and Its Problems* (Athens: Swallow Press and Ohio University Press, 1954).

20. *See* Jürgen Habermas, *Between Facts and Norms: Contributions to a Discourse Theory of Law and Democracy* (Cambridge, MA: MIT Press, 1996).

21. *See* Martha C. Nussbaum, *Women and Human Development: The Capabilities Approach* (Cambridge, UK: Cambridge University Press, 2000).

②

THEORETICAL BACKGROUND

In the 20th century, theorists in the field of public finance gave a precise definition of public goods. This definition claims that an ideal public good has two main qualities: its benefits are non-rival in consumption and it is non-excludable. Yet, few goods are purely public or purely private. Impure public goods also fall into two categories: they are either non-rival in consumption but excludable (club goods) or mostly non-excludable but rival in consumption (common pool resources).

In order to explain the approach to public goods that will be developed in this book, I will first explain how the idea of this book relates to the debate on public goods that has arisen since financial theorists developed a definition. *First*, I will go back to the technical definition of public goods that Musgrave and Samuelson developed within the framework of studies in public finance. I will also introduce some modifications and adjustments that have already been elaborated in public goods theories. This shall provide the background for defining what I will call a "public good." *Secondly*, I will introduce a new definition. This definition refers to the insights of economists, but interprets the characteristic properties of public goods slightly differently. It claims that public goods have to meet two conditions: There must be a minimum level of availability that is to be combined with conditions of open access. For interpreting these traits, it is crucial to discuss both the concept of *basic availability* and the concept of *open access* to some length.

Third, I shall give an explanation on how this type of goods relates to goods that have similarities with public goods and are sometimes even conflated with them: welfare goods, collective goods in the sense of state ownership, and the commons. *Fourth*, I will give a list of public goods that fall under the category of public goods in the sense I wish to employ in this volume. Even though this definition allows distinguishing between goods that deserve the name "public good" and other goods, it still provides a realm for a rich diversity of different things. It remains a characteristic trait of public goods theory that the category of a public good embraces a bundle of quite different things. Therefore, I shall also give an additional explanation on how such a broad list shall be narrowed down. The outcome is a list of types of goods that shall be discussed in this volume.

THE TECHNICAL DEFINITION RECONSIDERED

To explain the peculiarities of public goods, two starting points are likely to be chosen: Authors either start with the supply aspect or with the demand aspect. James Buchanan, for instance, focused on the peculiarity of public goods in categories of supply, more specifically, on goods that are jointly supplied.[1] One example of joint supply is one and the same producer offering both meat and leather as products taken from cows. They exploit the raw material in two different ways, yet profit from one source of production. In effect, the production costs are lower than they would be if both goods were produced separately. This advantage distorts the situation of competing for production costs, which are lower than they would be if each good was produced and offered according to the market laws. Yet, to approach goods exclusively on the supply-side is not satisfactory, for it cannot explain to a full extent the shortfalls that public goods regimes show in terms of resources allocation.

Therefore, Paul A. Samuelson and Richard A. Musgrave shifted the scope of analysis toward the category of demand. Both tried to elaborate a single criterion to distinguish public goods from goods that are provided by markets. Paul Samuelson states that one single attribute—jointness of consumption—accounts for dividing the world of produced goods into two classes: private-consumption goods and public-consumption goods. A situation like this has a very peculiar effect: In a setting that is purified from the influence of further factors, also called the *polar case*, the additional costs, which are caused by one additional user, amount to zero. The so-called *zero marginal cost* has a special effect: Consumers do not have to compete for public goods because additional benefits do not cause additional costs. This situation is best exemplified by a pure public good: domestic security. It makes no difference whether n or n + 1 person profit from domestic security. They rather will always enjoy the good to a degree that they wish to choose. Samuelson succeeded in giving an exact mathematical formula to this phenomenon and labelled it *non-rivalry*.

Yet in 1959, Richard Musgrave argued that another attribute is more important and captures the peculiarity of public goods more adequately than non-rivalry in consumption. According to his view, what really distinguishes public goods from private goods is whether or not a single potential user can effectively be excluded from benefits once the good is produced.[3] According to Musgrave's analysis, non-excludability is the most distinct characteristic of public goods. The classical example of a public good with this property is the lighthouse. Once the lighthouse is built, each boatswain who enters the port will profit from its existence; it is neither necessary nor possible to exclude anyone. Further examples comprise public space, domestic security, or infrastructure. Once these goods have been established, each person cannot only profit from them; persons even cannot be excluded from taking advantage of these goods. Musgrave, however, wanted to say this: Some goods actually cannot be protected from consumers because consumers cannot be excluded from the profits. Even if an institution aimed at reserving domestic security to some persons or to expel some persons from a public good, it would not succeed in doing so. According to this insight, public goods are non-excludable goods.

What both Musgrave and Samuelson tried to establish was a single criterion for the group of goods that are called *pure public goods* today. These cases are rare, under conditions of mass societies and scarcity of resources even more so. Nevertheless, some examples can be given: Domestic security is a pure public good. Some environmental goods match the criteria as well: Each person can profit from sunshine; and each person has access to the atmosphere and the air she is breathing. Yet, some further important public goods do not belong to the group of pure public goods. Education and science, health care and infrastructure are neither non-rival in consumption, nor are they non-excludable in the strict sense. As a consequence, several ideas have been introduced to add modifications without altogether giving up the crucial insights of both authors. Most important is the insight that both criteria for distinguishing public goods from private goods—non-excludability and non-rivalry—do not have to be taken as rival descriptions. Instead of relying on a single criterion, the combination of both provides a matrix that circumscribes four different cases, three of which count as public goods.

Table 2.1 shows that goods that are rival and excludable are clearly not public but private goods. Instead, goods that are non-rival and non-excludable can be called *pure public goods*.[4] As already indicated, these cases are rare, at least so in mass societies and under technological progress, which produces specific devices for exclusion. Much wider spread are *impure public goods*. They are to some degree either non-rival or non-excludable.

If goods are to a high degree non-rival, but excludable, they can be called *club goods*. Typical club goods are goods which are financed and sustained by a group of people with clearly defined membership rules. Within the group, the commonly provided goods are accessible to all. Examples are golf clubs that care for the lawn with free access to all members or private schools that educate all pupils who participate in funding the school services or religious communities with freely accessible services to members of that community. In these cases, benefits are reserved for members under non-competitive conditions.

Table 2.1. Types of Goods

	Rival	*Non-rival*
Excludable	Private Goods	Club Goods (= Impure Public Goods)
Non-excludable	Common Pool Resources (= Impure Public Goods)	Pure Public Goods

Yet, the group of club goods does not have to be restricted to clubs in the strict sense of the word. Instead, it suffices to combine the right to get access to a good with some definition of a group of people. There are further typical examples of goods whose access conditions are defined in terms of access barriers that define a community whose members are allowed to profit from the good without limitation: Sometimes entrance barriers are expressed in prices. As for public goods, these prices are not the result of market processes. They are rather defined as sources to fund a good that needs some entrance barrier to exclude non-payers. In this sense, public theaters can be organized as a club good. When consumers pay a fixed price and are then free to profit without limitation, they participate in a club good. Cultural goods, education, and health care would also be organized as club goods when rivalry could be excluded. Yet, to allow profits of users without limitation is normally not a realistic expectation. So, most impure cases of public goods in the sense of club goods are not non-rival in consumption in the strict sense. They are rather *to some degree* non-rival in consumption.

Table 2.1 also shows that goods which are non-excludable but rival are called *common pool resources*. Again, pure cases are rare. The best examples are still natural resources such as fishing grounds. Non-excludability means that there are no defined access barriers such as fishing licences, for instance. More realistic examples comprise public space or infrastructure. As long as no toll stations are built, highways and public space are non-excludable; yet, congestion demonstrates rivalry over that good.

However, perfect non-excludability is rare. There are a bundle of different obstacles that have to be taken into account. As for natural resources, access barriers can be defined in terms of property rights. Furthermore, natural obstacles to profit from a common pool resource must be taken into account. Even though a water reservoir may be theoretically accessible to potential beneficiaries, it might not practically be accessible due to the fact that the distance between the person and the reservoir is too long. In other words, in most cases, some access barriers will exist. And there will always be persons who are not in a situation to cope with these barriers. Because of these insights, common pool resources are normally categorized as *highly non-excludable*.

For public goods theory, it is critical to see the latter point: It is not correct to say that public goods altogether lack access barriers. Some authors claim that taking into account this insight suffices to cope with one of the most popular critiques of public goods.

In 1968, Garrett Hardin published an article entitled "The Tragedy of the Commons."[5] According to his view, public goods are peculiarly prone to a "tragedy of the commons," because collectively used goods such as common land, common fishing pools, national parks, and even welfare goods are self-destructive systems. A pasture open to every person will invite herdsmen to over exploit the soil; unlimited access to the sea and to national parks destroys productivity and beauty; and promises made by welfare states stimulate irresponsible behavior. In short, "freedom in a commons brings ruin to all."[6] These comments draw attention to an important point: If non-excludability means that there are no entrance barriers at all, public goods are an endangered group of goods indeed. In my view, this comment does not necessarily say that public goods need to be surrounded by wisely chosen access barriers. Instead, it suggests that the categories of non-rivalry as well as non-excludability are imprecise. They need to be reinterpreted.

A DEFINITION OF PUBLIC GOODS

According to public goods theories, public goods fall into three categories. They are either pure public goods or impure public goods and the group of impure public goods splits into two subgroups, for those are either common pool resources or club goods. Instead of splitting the group of public goods into pure public goods, that rarely exist, and two subgroups, I will give a definition of public goods that takes into account both features of public goods. Instead of placing the emphasis on one of the characteristics, I shall develop a hybrid test for public goods. They need to share both characteristics to count as public goods. Furthermore, I will reinterpret both features so that both criteria have a slightly different meaning without giving up the initial insight.

So, my approach to a definition of public goods has two aspects. *First*, instead of separating the tests proposed by Samuelson and Musgrave and instead of distinguishing different types of public goods (pure public goods, club goods, common pool resources), I shall develop a hybrid test that counts for all public goods. It combines both characteristics that Musgrave and Samuelson once developed. *Secondly*, the concepts of non-excludability and non-rivalry will be interpreted in a new way. In my view, they give two criteria that a good must both meet to count as a public good: There is a non-competitive level of availability of that good for each person; and the access conditions to that minimum level are non-selective in the sense of giving each person the same opportunity to participate in that good. I shall abbreviate the first condition as the "basic availability condition"; the second condition as the "open access condition." Together they define conditions of fair access. This is the property that distinguishes public goods from other types of goods. In the remainder of this section I shall explain this interpretation of a "public good" in detail.

To call something a good implies that individuals appreciate this item and that they are interested in benefiting from its existence. In this sense, the notion of a good is quite unspecific. Persons enjoy goods for different motives and reasons: They wish to consume goods or they like to possess them; they utilize goods or appreciate their aesthetic value. Some philosophers tend to put more meaning into the term of a good. Michael Walzer, i.e., argues that goods are constituted by communities.[7] This draws a close connection between the concept of a good and a more precise idea of what its value consists in. So, we might distinguish between economic, aesthetic, and communal goods. For my approach to public goods, it suffices to take the meaning of "a good" in the very loose sense of an item that serves the interests of individuals. To call something a public good adds two further conditions. To explain these conditions, I shall start with the ideas which in my view explain the concepts of non-rivalry and non-excludability best. I shall then discuss how I wish to interpret both of them.

To call a good *non-rival* in consumption says that each person can profit from the good to an amount that satisfies his or her desires without distracting benefits from any other person. This has two implications. *First*, non-rivalry means that the profit of one person does not relate to the profit of any other person. More precisely, there is no competition over a shared resource. *Secondly*, it says that a good is plenty. In many cases, this second assumption is unrealistic. Yet, it is still reasonable to say that it is a characteristic feature of public goods that they do not imply the normal patterns of competition. This provides the background for an interpretation of non-rivalry that slightly modifies its initial content. Non-rivalry does not primarily say that there is no competition at all. It rather says that *up to a certain point that needs to be defined for each good separately, each person has access to the same amount and the same type of benefits.* I shall term this first criterion the *basic availability condition.*[8]

I shall now turn to the second defining feature of public goods. To say that public goods are *non-excludable* has already been criticized as often being conflated with the idea of a lack of entrance barriers. In my view, non-excludability does *not* say that entrance barriers do not exist. The important point is rather that each person who wishes to profit from a public good can do so. Entrance barriers are not established along criteria that define a group of persons who will profit from a good in advance. In other words, *entrance barriers are not combined with selective criteria that define a list of potential beneficiaries and exclude others.* In this specified sense public goods are open access regimes. Accordingly, I shall call this second condition the *open access condition.*

This second condition needs some comments. It does *not* imply that the realistic expectations to participate in a public good are always the same. There might be reasons why some persons might be in a better position to participate in a public good. A highway might be close to their home; a public space might be in their reach; they might be in a position to need participation in a public good and as a consequence they will make the required effort to participate. Other people might be lucky in the sense that they do not need to participate in a particular public good. In short, the open access condition does *not* imply that *no* entrance barriers exist. Instead, these entrance barriers are defined in an impartial manner.

Finally, both conditions must be put together to define a good as a public good. Together they circumscribe conditions of *fair access.* As for a public good, no potential beneficiary will be excluded for arbitrary reasons. Moreover, each person can participate in the profits of a public good to some reasonable degree.

To summarize the argument, two conditions that a public good must meet simultaneously have been outlined. They are called the basic availability condition and the open access condition. They can be summarized in the following way:

- *Basic availability condition*: To some reasonable degree, benefits accrue to each person who wishes to profit from a good under non-competitive conditions.
- *Open access condition*: Entrance barriers that regulate access to a good are not combined with criteria which define a list of potential beneficiaries and exclude others.

TYPES OF COLLECTIVE GOODS

The term "public good" is sometimes used in an unspecified way. Indeed, some groups of goods have similarities with public goods, but according to our definition can be distinguished from public goods in the strict sense. In this chapter I wish to lay emphasis on the differences between public goods and three further groups of goods: welfare goods, state property, and collective goods.

First, public goods in the sense defined can be distinguished from welfare goods. The concept of *welfare good* must in some way be spelled out in terms of social justice. Welfare goods might also be restricted to a minimal provision, so that at first glance, welfare goods seem similar to public goods in this respect. Yet, to build in criteria of social justice to give access to a good like education or health care is not compatible with the open access condition. A public good must be open to all potential users in the strict sense; a welfare good on the other hand has a specified range of beneficiaries.

A *second* distinguishing feature is that the concept of the welfare good has a distinct normative implication. Welfare goods serve aims of social justice; the range of goods that meet this condition cannot be determined without first exploring reasons for social justice. This means that welfare goods are defined in normative terms. Public goods, on the other hand, do not rely on normative presumptions. The definition does not imply that public goods serve social aims, nor does it imply that public goods should exist; it rather draws on peculiarities of a group of goods that can be spelled out in descriptive terms. Thus, the definition posits that whenever a good meets the conditions of basic availability and open access, it can be called a "public good." The question of whether or not institutions should invest in public goods can be separated from their definition. I shall address the normative questions in the remainder of this volume; for now it is important to notice that the concept itself does not have normative implications.

The definition of a public good does not collapse into the idea of *state ownership* either. It is an intriguing feature of public goods theory that questions of ownership can be distinguished both from the definition of public goods and from the theoretical implications. Usually, questions of ownership come into the picture when authors turn to the question of how public goods can best be sustained. As goods that do not fit into market structures, they need support through public finance. Yet, even at that point of discussion, several theoretical decisions can still be argued for. Even though it is correct to say that public goods do not fit into market structures, it is not necessarily the case that public goods need to be upheld by means of public finance.[9] Yet, it is not my aim to argue for a theory of public finance. Instead I hope that pointing out the reasons why public goods serve democratic societies might suffice as a motivation for private businesses and private persons as well as for political institutions to invest in public goods.

Third, public goods are distinguished from *the commons*. This group of goods is another type of collective goods that is situated within groups of people or whole societies who both care for that good and profit from it.[10] Two differences are obvious. *First*, public goods do not deserve their name because they are situated in societies in terms of collective norms and shared normative ideas about these goods. To call them public *goods* starts with the idea that persons profit from their services. Furthermore, the definition of a public good suggests that each person who wishes to benefit from it can to some degree actually do so. The meaning of a good as a public good is not derived from values that a community attributes to it. The concept of a good starts with the idea of benefits that accrue to profiteers, but without identifying a specific value inherent in the object. *Secondly*, collective norms in dealing with that item are not central to the concept of a public good. Instead, the criterion for calling goods public is their character of offering benefits to those who wish to enjoy them.

This does not say that rules of good practice cannot be established. Instead, in establishing a public good, it might be reasonable to introduce rules how beneficiaries should treat that good when they gain access to it. But this is not to say that the good deserves its name because individuals employ a certain range of norms in profiting from it.

A LIST OF PUBLIC GOODS

It is one peculiarity of public goods theory to deal with a range of goods that is not only vast, but also very mixed. When being asked about what counts as a public good, people are likely to name the items listed below:

> Shared knowledge, public education, the sciences, a health-care system, traffic infrastructure, the media, the cyberspace, the landscape, public space, natural resources like clean air and water, the seas, the sun, climate stability, cultural heritage, peace, harmony, inner and outer security, the judicial system, shared knowledge, public sanitation, sewerage, the financial system, financial stability, global justice.

In this section I wish to present a more conclusive list of public goods. Therefore, I shall first give three additional criteria that help narrow down the range of goods that I wish to explore in this volume, resulting in a list of central types of public goods. The additional criteria are that the public goods I shall deal with are (1) tangible, not intangible; (2) final, not intermediate; and (3) public goods regimes, not public goods alone.

1. *Tangible, not intangible*: A first factor that restricts the list of public goods results from the distinction between real objects and objects that cannot be easily expressed in terms of physical properties. Harmony and peace might have the properties of public goods. Yet, they are ideas that can be realized in many different ways. The public goods that I wish to deal with have a physical existence. Usually, one can describe them as entities with characteristic physical properties. To express this, I wish to divide the group of public goods in a group of *tangible* and a group of *intangible goods*. The goods I will deal with in this book are tangible goods.

2. *Final, not intermediate*: Following a proposal of Kaul, Grunberg, and Stern, public goods can be divided into *final public goods* and *intermediate public goods*.[11] One irritating fact in public goods theories is that the provision of public goods sometimes presupposes that institutions are available that share public good features themselves. This group of institutions can be termed "intermediate public goods" in that they share some characteristics of public goods, yet simultaneously provide a necessary background for the organization of tangible public goods such as education, public space, or domestic security.

   Intermediary public goods comprise a group of institutions such as a legal and financial system as well as democratic institutions. The patterns of distributions of benefits are indeed comparable to the structure of public goods: A stable financial system is profitable for each citizen; and its benefits are not reserved for a special group of beneficiaries. Nevertheless, I wish to exclude this second layer of public goods from my discussion. Two reasons are central to this decision. *First*, intermediary public goods are less specific in what they bring about. To support public goods and help to realize them is only one function of these institutions. Often, they serve the common good in many different ways. *Secondly*, intermediary public goods can be distinguished from the public goods that I wish to discuss in primarily serving a society, but not citizens with a range of different needs and desires. As a result of these thoughts, the judicial system and the financial system will not be on my list.
3. *Regimes, not items*: A third factor to shorten the list results from the distinction between a public good as a solitary physical thing and a public goods regime. Unlike other types of goods, the profit from a public good is not immediately related to its utilization or its consumption. A car is something that is being used by its owner; food is being consumed. Yet, a water resource, a public space, and a health care system remain stable when being used. In placing emphasis on the character of public goods as regimes I also wish to stress that the characteristic features of public goods usually result from the interconnectedness of many single instantiations of a complex good and an organization that supports the existence of the system. In my discussion of public goods, I do not wish to speak about single

> things such as a street; nor do I wish to abstract from the fact that a public good needs some type of management or internal organization. So, instead of talking about single entities I wish to discuss the regimes that comprise distinct modes of organization as well as the localized instantiation of a public good itself that delivers the services and benefits that persons wish to enjoy. These are the reasons why the study is focused on public goods regimes.
>
> Moreover, the relation between regime and benefit is not a random one. To call a street a public good does not only imply that there is a street that people can use, but it means that streets are organized in a way that guarantees their structure as a public good. Furthermore, in some sense of the word "typical benefits" can be outlined. Those who profit from streets normally wish to make use of them when travelling or moving from one place to another. One could imagine that each person could profit from air in terms of throwing balls through it; but no one would therefore call air a public good, because the benefits are atypical. For relating typical benefits to a single public good, it is helpful to take the whole regime in account.

As an effect of these three additional criteria, some items from the initial list must be expelled because they are not tangible (condition a). Those are peace, stability in terms of financial stability, and global justice. Some further goods can be excluded from the list because they are not final, but intermediary public goods (condition b): the judicial system and the financial system. Others can be expelled because they do not represent public goods as regimes: the sun and the seas are items rather than regimes.

After having applied these additional criteria to the initial list, seven types of public goods can be listed:

1. *Inner and outer security*
2. *Infrastructure*
3. *Education and science*
4. *Environmental goods*
5. *Public space*
6. *Cultural goods*
7. *Institutions of care*

Each of these items can be realized in a way that fits the criteria for a public good. They can be organized according to the conditions of basic availability and of open access. In that case, no person will be excluded from a basic level of benefits for arbitrary reasons.

In public goods theory it is crucial to work on realistic examples without losing sight of the theoretical premises. Therefore, the distinction between types and tokens is helpful. A token is a concrete realization of a type of thing. A type, on the other hand, is an abstract category that emphasizes the central properties of an object. In order to give a more precise picture of the range of public goods, I shall also present a list of tokens of public goods. The examples for tokens are not intended to cover all possible items; they rather figure as exemplifications of the types of public goods.

1. *Inner and outer security*: a system of institutions of security that comprise a well-equipped and well-organized army, an office of defense and a police force.
2. *Infrastructure*: traffic infrastructure that comprises free highways, public transportation, airways and airports; sewers and public sanitation; the Internet, television, and devices of telecommunication; broadcasting, print media.
3. *Education and science:* public schools and universities, libraries, institutions of shared knowledge (including scientific communities that make their results public).
4. *Environmental goods:* clean air and water, fishing grounds, national parks.
5. *Public space:* streets and sidewalks, city parks, landscape.
6. *Cultural goods:* theaters and operas, public events, literature that is collected in libraries, and the Internet, buildings, and landscapes that figure as cultural heritage.
7. *Institutions of care:* a basic public health care system including hospitals; institutions of child care; nursing homes.

NOTES

1. *See* James M. Buchanan, *Public Finance in Democratic Process: Fiscal Institutions and the Individual Choice* (Chapel Hill: University of North Caro-

lina Press, 1967), 11ff. For a discussion of financial aspects of the public goods problems *see also*: James M. Buchanan, *The Demand and Supply of Public Goods* (Chicago: Chicago University Press, 1968).

2. *See* Paul A. Samuelson, "Pure Theory of Public Expenditure and Taxation," in *Public Economics: An Analysis of Public Production and Consumption and Their Relations to the Private Sectors*, ed. by Julius Margolis and Henri Guitton (London et al.: Macmillan, 1969), 107–110.

3. Richard A. Musgrave, *The Theory of Public Finance: A Study in Public Economy* (New York et al.: McGraw-Hill, 1959), 8 and 387–389.

4. A similar table is provided by Inge Kaul, Isabelle Grunberg, and Marc A. Stern, "Defining Global Public Goods," in *Global Public Goods: International Cooperation in the 21st Century* (New York and Oxford: Oxford University Press, 1999), 5.

5. Garrett Hardin, "The Tragedy of the Commons," *Science* 162, no. 3859 (1968): 1243–1248.

6. Hardin, *The Tragedy*, 1244.

7. Michael Walzer, *Spheres of Justice: A Defense of Pluralism and Equality* (New York: Basic Books, 1983).

8. This interpretation also fits the concept of "public" in its general meaning. When something is termed "public," this means that it is not restricted to private use.

9. I shall discuss this point in chapter 8 in more detail.

10. *See* Elinor Ostrom, *Governing the Commons: The Evolution of Institutions for Collective Action* (Cambridge, UK, and New York: Cambridge University Press, 1990).

11. Kaul, Grunberg, and Stern, *Global Public Goods*, 13.

3

PROBLEMS OF SUPPLY RECONSIDERED

For many decades, public goods have been a subject of research in financial studies. Since James M. Buchanan, Richard A. Musgrave, and Paul E. Samuelson conceptualized the peculiarity of public goods as non-excludable and non-rivalrous goods,[1] public goods have primarily been discussed regarding problems of supply. As a consequence, they have more generally been regarded as "troublemakers." In a market economy, public goods cause major failures and misallocations of resources. Due to their characteristics, public goods have distorting effects on the allocation of resources and on the match between demand and supply in the market. In addition, they foster so-called collective action problems. Confronted with the choice of either participating in the provision of public goods or profiting from them for free, consumers will prefer the latter whenever it is possible. Worse yet, the temptation to behave as a free-rider and to show uncooperative behavior are emblematic for public goods regimes. In public goods regimes, suboptimal outcomes are considered the tragic results of perfectly rational choices.

All these considerations focus on the aspect of supply. Public goods need to be established and maintained. In particular, they need to be financed. Precisely because problems that are caused by the structure of public goods have to be taken seriously, I shall first present some of the resulting shortfalls. My presentation in this chapter, however, is not restricted to these problems. I rather wish to combine some central claims with a critical reassessment. I am particularly interested in how the problems related to public goods regimes in the classic sense relate to the definition of public goods that was given in chapter two. The overall aim of this chapter is not to present an alternative approach to public goods. I rather wish to prepare the argument of this book in reassessing doctrines about public goods that still dominate the discourse on public goods.

MARKET FAILURES

Due to their characteristic, public goods provoke market failures. In this section I shall introduce into the distorting effects of public goods that occur in a market economy; I also shall develop some counterarguments. Even though resulting problems have to be taken seriously, there is no reason *not* to add another perspective on public goods and markets. According to that view, public goods do also have a positive effect on market economies. Again, I shall start with the "classic view."

Acquiring and consuming goods is one thing, producing them another. It was once regarded a miracle how both sides—demand and supply—eventually fit together, even in generating wealth, so that everyone is better off through a system of voluntary asset exchange. A theoretical explanation for the possibility of this outcome was given in the midst of the last century; its core is the pricing mechanism. All the information that is needed to make the system work is encapsulated in the price of commodities. The price can be linked to the sphere of consumers in that it expresses how much consumers are willing to increase or decrease their spending in relation to other commodities within a basket of goods. It is simultaneously linked to the sphere of production in that producers compete for the reduction of production costs so that their offer meets the conditions which are set by the consumers. Competition between different suppliers supports the convergence toward the point where demand and supply meet. Under conditions of perfect competition and free-floating information, consumers would get what they want at best prices, and resources would be allocated so that this outcome would be produced.[2] This is a simplified version of what "efficiency" means and how the "pricing mechanism" works.

For the discussion of public goods, it is critical to acknowledge that the performances of the market rely on an undistorted pricing mechanism. And exactly this cannot be guaranteed when commodities have the characteristics of public goods in the classic sense of non-excludable and non-rival goods. If no consumer can be excluded, the informational link between consumer's choices, acceptance of prices for the commodity and supply is interrupted. As a consequence, neither the provision of an adequate range of goods, nor the best possible allocation of resources can be guaranteed or will be the natural outcome according to market laws. Instead, there will be an over- or under supply of public goods and as a consequence an artificial cost-bearing system will be needed, for instance a system of public finance. Subsidies in turn lower the prices, public goods turn into monopolies.

This illustration may suffice to give an overview of the problems that public goods in the classic sense will cause in a market economy. Yet, research on public goods and financial techniques has gone beyond an investigation of negative side effects. It could also be shown that some negative effects of public goods regimes can be mitigated.[3] An artificial stimulation of competitiveness between private suppliers can be achieved if systems of incentives in terms of rewards for excellent contributions can be established. Economic laws can also be simulated in public goods regimes to a certain degree. Information about consumers' desires can be collected, it can substitute real demand curves, and contribute to what Stiglitz calls "efficiency conditions for public goods."[4] Simulations like this help to a certain degree even though the distortion of market laws cannot fully be eradicated.

In discussing public goods in our sense of the term, the first question that has to be answered is whether or not the same effects will occur. Since competition is reduced to the sphere of a good beyond what I call the "basic level" of benefits, pricing mechanisms actually cannot unfold. They presuppose real patterns of competition. In addition, access barriers different from those set by the market have a distorting effect on economic laws. This leads to the conclusion that goods that meet the open access condition and the basic availability condition will also have distorting effects on markets. Nevertheless, there are some strategies at hand to cope with the resulting problems.

One way of coping with distorting effects of public goods regimes on a theoretical level is the argument that efficiency is not a trump value. Efficiency is an important trait of exchange systems; it simply is the best achievable outcome for consumers in that products match the bundles of goods that individuals wish to acquire to optimal prices. Yet, if consumers had to choose between a bundle of goods whose production can fully meet efficiency standards and therefore cannot include a public good and a bundle of goods that include a selection of public goods which do not meet efficiency standards, I doubt that they would necessarily choose the first.

Another way of coping with the problematic properties of public goods regarding the aspect of supply starts with questioning the bad impact of public goods on a more comprehensive level. This argument states that if public goods actually had detrimental economic effects, nation-states that sustain public goods would necessarily suffer from a bad economic performance, too. Yet, the truth is that welfare states do quite well in terms of overall economic performance.[5] It is not easy to measure the precise impact of public goods on that result, but there is evidence that they even support market economies.

In a recent contribution, Peter H. Lindert argues that even direct social transfers do not have a bad effect on economic performance; quite the opposite appears to be true. In *Growing Public* Lindert explores the links between economic growth and social policies that redistribute income—among them are the expenses for health care and schools.[6] One of the most astonishing findings of his study, which comprises a unique collection of data about social spending, says: "Among the OECD countries, the period with the fastest-growing welfare states—between 1950 and 1980—included history's best-ever golden age of growth (1950–1973), even though it also included the oil shocks that hit in 1973 and 1979."[7] Even though growth is always due to many factors, one general conclusion can be drawn: "The net national costs of social transfers, and of the taxes that finance them, are essentially zero."[8]

The examples that Lindert provides are examples of how costs and benefits are interrelated when states provide goods as welfare goods. Nevertheless, a lesson can also be learned regarding public goods. Public goods are different from welfare goods.[9] But what they have in common is that monetary sources apart from the exchange mechanisms of markets become necessary. Even though Lindert points to a complex link between taxes, net social transfer, and economic performances, and even though his study is focused on a specific period of time, acknowledging the fact that providing welfare goods does not deviate from an overall good economic performance might be helpful. At least, the general statement that public goods disturb markets to a degree that economic damage must be expected can be denied.

In the remainder of this paragraph I shall go one step further and introduce the idea that the provision of public goods might help market economies to flourish. The claims I shall present are not conclusive in the sense of demonstrating a direct economic value of public goods. The examples I shall choose might rather contribute to questioning an overall negative economic narrative on public goods.

The first thing to notice is that some goods that share public goods features have already been welcomed by authors that all in all were convinced of the superiority of a laissez-faire style economy. An example is the treatment of infrastructure and education in the writings of Adam Smith.[10] He argues for subsidies for infrastructure, in particular so when that good facilitates commerce. Goods which are not directly related to facilitating commerce also should be supported by means of public finance as far as they can be considered ancillary to economic development and economic progress. This means that problems resulting from public goods features of a good can be outweighed by evaluating their profits.

Milton Friedman also argues in favor of a range of public goods being provided by political institutions, even though he generally argues against government intervention.[11] Friedman argues in favor of governmental subsidies for elementary school and liberal art colleges. Among his arguments is the increase of "economic productivity" of students.[12] Another type of argument relates to the insight in "neighborhood effects." Neighborhood effects arise "when actions of individuals have effects on other individuals for which it is not feasible to charge or recompense them."[13] Enforcement of appropriate compensation is either not possible or not feasible. Pollution of waterways, highways, and parks are among the examples that Friedman discusses.[14] Although arguments from neighborhood effects "can be a reason for limiting the activities of government as well as for expanding them,"[15] as for environmental goods, they provide arguments for governmental engagement in public goods.

Besides arguments that relate to economic productivity and neighborhood effects, one might argue that public goods support economic performances. Public goods contribute to the market in that they provide opportunities for individuals to get connected with each other. More precisely, public goods provide that type of connection that markets need to develop: they connect individuals without introducing any selective effect. This results from the open access condition.

A good example to illustrate this point is the impact that the railway had for the development of the city of Chicago as an economically flourishing city. Since the end of the 19th century, the railway has provided something like a physical backbone for this city. Until today, traffic infrastructure has stimulated and structured economic development. Railways do not necessarily constitute a public good. But in the case of the Chicago railway, they serve as an example of the open access condition insofar as each person who wishes to profit from that good actually can use it. In "A City Reinvents Itself," William A. Testa argues that the infrastructure and its specific features have been a key factor not only for economic success, but also for the paths of how Chicago has developed into what today presents itself as a global city.[16] Another recent example for the immense effect of a public good on markets is the Internet.[17] Imagine the Internet as a private good. This could result in the effect that it would no longer be usable by each person who wishes to do so. Markets, instead, need background conditions that do not have selective effects.

GROUP SIZE AND MOTIVATION

A general theory on public goods as non-excludable and non-rival goods does not only point to distorting effects on markets. Another focus of attention has been a set of problems of collective action. One central problem is a behavior that has been described as "free-riding."[18] In 1965, Mancur Olson explains that participants of small-size groups are more likely to be motivated to voluntarily contribute to the sustenance of common goods than the participants of larger groups. Instead, members of large groups are more likely to indulge in free-riding whenever it is possible.[19] When public goods are considered as truly non-exclusive goods, this is a severe flaw. In fact, Olson laid the grounds for a common doctrine on public goods which still dominates the discourse on public goods. It says that whenever possible, individuals choose the behavior of self-interested profiteers without being ready to contribute to public goods regimes voluntarily.

After years of further research in how people react to public goods, there still seems to be some truth in Olson's analysis. Yet, in some respects it could be reduced to a more realistic assessment that also introduces differentiation. What could, e.g., be shown is that group-size is only one factor among others that have an impact on motivation. Particularly, it is not an absolute factor, but rather a factor whose strength correlates with whether or not other factors are also given.[20] If a good is highly non-rival and depends on the contributions of the beneficiaries for its provision, group sizes can even have a positive effect on the probability of provision. The level of resources provided to support public radio, for instance, will be greater when a larger rather than a smaller population can be called upon.[21]

Knowledge and information about the situation also appear to be crucial. The motivation to voluntarily contribute to costs is correlated to what the contributors actually know about the impact of their contribution—the transparency of payment systems—and whether or not the contribution has an impact on the production of the good.[22] A further factor that strengthens motivation to contribute to public goods is knowledge about the production function. The production function can have different shapes. Knowledge of critical points that have to be reached unless the good can be provided sometimes is sufficient to motivate people to participate in voluntary contributions.[23] In short, progress in game theory has led to a much more finely grained and differentiated picture regarding the problem of free-riding in classic public goods theory. The critique of Olson's dogma says that an overall statement is not possible unless a much more fine-grained approach to the knowledge and information of the beneficiaries is also taken into account.

COLLECTIVE CHOICE: CAUGHT IN A TRAP?

Besides the problem of free-riding, negative side effects of public goods regimes are illustrated in comparison to the prisoner's dilemma.

It describes a setting of two imprisoned individuals that both make a perfectly rational choice and end up with a tragic result.[24] As for public goods theory, the paradox which the dilemma illustrates is not only that the individually rational choice leads to apparently irrational outcomes. Allegedly, the situation can also directly be translated into a public goods scenario. Think of two individuals who both need a street in front of their home. The best strategy to get the street would be to invest money in the street project. But instead, each person only considers his own advantage and, this is an important part of the story, does not trust the other person. If the "penalties" were distributed as they are in the prisoner's dilemma—we can for a moment translate them as higher or lower prices in building the street—the best strategy for both and the lowest penalty would be to cooperate. Yet, both neighbors choose differently.

Let us presuppose for a moment that it makes sense to regard the situation through the lenses of persons who think strategically and who primarily wish to yield the best results for themselves. Even then it can be argued that the scenario does not perfectly fit a public goods scenario. In our street example, it could also be the case that without resources to rely on external intervention, individuals get together and start bargaining. However, the conclusion will not be that people always start cooperating.

In the prisoner's scenario, the participants cannot communicate with each other and therefore they cannot negotiate the situation. This assumption correlates with the assumption that the choice for either cooperative or uncooperative behavior will only be made after the situation and the penalties have already been fixed. When public goods regimes are compared to the prisoner's dilemma, two things are taken for granted: Neither are the competences of individuals to negotiate with each other a reliable option; nor do we need to take seriously the functions of public institutions and democratic devices. Even though, so far, we have not discussed how the properties of public goods in the sense of the basic availability condition and the open access condition translate into the precise nature of the regime, it is apparent that public goods do not respond to solitary claims of individuals. They rather respond to interests of masses of individuals. At least in some cases, they are in a situation to negotiate conditions of supply; and they can also be imagined to have access to information that helps form an idea about the level of contribution that each person can be expected to make.

Nevertheless, public goods pose problems of supply. One of the reasons is that they are different from collective goods in the sense of goods that are situated within a normative setting, within a community.

Elinor Ostrom examines various examples that demonstrate the capacity of communities to invent rules that serve both aims: protecting the commons and giving each person access to them.[25] Yet, the examples that Ostrom discusses all must be considered collective goods. They comprise communal tenures of meadows and forests in Törbel, Switzerland, common pool resources in Japanese villages, irrigation institutions in Spain, Turkey, and the Philippines and the collective management of common fishing grounds in various regions of the world. Nevertheless, Ostrom's study makes an important point for a theoretical assessment of public goods as well. She shows that institutions of control and enforcement are a very effective way of regulating access and support for collective goods. There is no reason why this should not also apply to public goods. This would help prevent the dilemmas that result from a situation in which those institutions have not been developed.

GETTING THE CRITIQUE RIGHT

In this chapter I have focused on some points that are central to a widespread narrative on public goods. As for the picture of public goods as "troublemakers," it is not my aim to play down the problems that are analyzed in financial studies and in collective action analysis. Instead, I have argued that, for reasons of fairness, the whole picture must be presented. Public goods also support markets and serve as door-openers for industrial development. Moreover, I have not tried to question the findings of Olson that group size relates to the willingness to contribute to public goods. Yet, it is fair to say that further factors help modify the behavior of consumers. Information appears to be central. Knowledge about the range of consumers and about the production function has an impact on motivation as well. Finally, the comparison between public goods and the situation of a prisoner's dilemma does not completely convince. It overlooks the reality and the possibility of individuals to negotiate. Without the possibility of making contracts, not only public goods, but also exchange mechanisms regarding private goods would be at stake.

My critical assessment, however, does not end at this point. A fundamental limitation of the perspective which has been presented so far results from the treatment of public goods as just another kind of goods which have to be distinguished from "normal" consumption goods. As a consequence from that perspective, the classic approach focuses on one side of public goods regimes: their peculiarities in the market. In the remainder of this book, I shall switch to a different perspective by situating public goods in political theory.

NOTES

1. James M. Buchanan, *Public Finance in Democratic Process: Fiscal Institutions and the Individual Choice* (Chapel Hill: University of North Carolina Press, 1967); James M. Buchanan, *The Demand and Supply of Public Goods* (Chicago: Chicago University Press, 1968); Richard A. Musgrave, *The Theory of Public Finance: A Study in Public Economy* (New York et al.: McGraw-Hill Book Company, 1959); Paul A. Samuelson, "The Pure Theory of Public Expenditure," in *Public Economics: An Analysis of Public Production and Consumption and Their Relations to the Private Sectors*, ed. by Julius Margolis and Henri Guitton (London et al.: Macmillan, 1969), 98–123.

2. An explanation of market and welfare efficiency is given by Amartya Sen in "Markets and Freedoms," in *Rationality and Freedom* (Cambridge, MA, and London, England: Belknap Press of Harvard University Press, 2002), 504–505.

3. Throughout the discussion, it must also be taken into account that theories about efficiency rely on highly idealized conditions, most of which can rarely be met in reality. One of these conditions is perfect information. Another condition is perfect competitiveness that presupposes the non-existence of entrance barriers to markets. Joseph E. Stiglitz gives a detailed critique of the two basic theorems of welfare economics in: *Whither Socialism?* (Cambridge, MA, and London, England: MIT Press, 1994). Stiglitz argues that the assumption of perfect information has to be substituted by ideas about imperfect information. Incentives and competition play a far more important role for good economic performances than accounted for by welfare economics. In effect, the gap between public goods regimes and processes in private markets diminishes.

4. Joseph E. Stiglitz, *Economics of the Public Sector* (2nd ed., New York and London: W.W. Norton & Company, 1988), 131–140.

5. *See* Fritz W. Scharpf, "Economic Changes, Vulnerabilities, and Institutional Capabilities," in *Welfare and Work in the Open Economy, Vol. 1: From Vulnerability to Competitiveness*, ed. Fritz W. Scharpf and Vivien A. Schmidt (Oxford and New York: Oxford University Press, 2000), 21–124.

6. Peter H. Lindert, *Growing Public. Social Spending and Economic Growth since the Eighteenth Century, Vol. 1: The Story* (Cambridge, UK, and New York: Cambridge University Press, 2004).

7. Lindert, *Growing Public*, 30.

8. Lindert, *Growing Public*, 29.

9. For this, *see* chapter two, section "Types of Collective Goods."

10. Adam Smith, *An Inquiry into the Nature and Causes of the Wealth of Nations*, ed. Edwin Cannan (Chicago: University of Chicago Press, 1976), 213–337.

11. Milton Friedman, *Capitalism and Freedom* (Chicago and London: University of Chicago Press, 2002), 177–189.

12. Friedman, *Capitalism and Freedom*, 88.

13. Friedman, *Capitalism and Freedom*, 30.

14. Friedman, *Capitalism and Freedom*, 30ff. and 88.

15. Friedman, *Capitalism and Freedom*, 31.

16. William A. Testa, "A City Reinvents Itself," in *Global Chicago*, ed. Charles Madigan (Urbana and Chicago: Chicago Council on Foreign Relations University of Illinois Press, 2004), 35–69.

17. For the importance of national governmental policies regarding the Internet *see* Cass R. Sunstein, *republic.com* (3rd ed., Princeton and Oxford: Princeton University Press, 2002), 132–134.

18. See Anthony De Jasay, *Social Contract, Free Ride: A Study of the Public Goods Problem* (Oxford: Clarendon Press, 1989).

19. *See* Mancur Olson, *The Logic of Collective Action: Public Goods and the Theory of Groups* (20th ed., Cambridge, MA, and London, England: Harvard University Press, 2002). Olson says: "In a small group in which a member gets such a large fraction of the total benefit that he would be better off if he paid the entire cost himself, rather than go without the good, there is some presumption that the collective good will be provided. In a group in which no one member got such a large benefit from the collective good that he had an interest in providing it even if he had to pay all of the cost, but in which the individual was still so important in terms of the whole group that his contribution or lack of contribution to the group objective had a noticeable effect on the costs or benefits of others in the group, the result is indeterminate. By contrast, in a large group in which no single individual's contribution makes a perceptible difference to the group as a whole, or the burden or benefit of any

single member of the group, it is certain that a collective good will *not* be provided unless there is coercion or some outside inducements that will lead the members of the large group to act in their common interest." Olson, *Collective Action*, 44. Italics by Olson.

20. *See* Elinor Ostrom, "Property-Rights Regimes and Common Goods: A Complex Link," in *Reinventing European and International Governance*, ed. Adrienne Héritier (Lanham, Boulder, New York, and Oxford: Rowman & Littlefield, 2002), 29–57.

21. Ostrom, *Property-Rights Regimes*, 32.

22. Ostrom, *Property-Rights Regimes*, 36.

23. A particular shape of the production function, which can be described as step-level function, even is sufficient for preventing free-riding in the first place. Step-level functions have the characteristic not to react in terms of production unless a critical amount of costs have been provided. *See* Ostrom, *Property-Rights Regimes*, 35–36.

24. For a short summary of the history of the prisoner's dilemma in game theory and an application to public goods theory, *see* Ian Malcolm David Little, *Ethics, Economics, and Politics: Principles of Public Policy* (New York and Oxford: Oxford University Press, 2002), 89–100.

25. Elinor Ostrom, *Governing the Commons: The Evolution of Institutions for Collective Action* (Cambridge, UK, and New York: Cambridge University Press, 1990) and Elinor Ostrom et al., "Revisiting the Commons: Local Lessons, Global Challenges," *Science* 284 (1999): 278–282.

4

GENERATING THE PUBLIC

In theorizing the public sphere, the acknowledgments of specific preconditions have already played an important role. The public sphere does not spring unconditionally from societies nor does it reproduce itself unconditionally. Both Jürgen Habermas and Michael Warner acknowledge the importance of print media for the birth of the public.[1] Recently, Cass R. Sunstein argued that the roles of Internet and television should not be underestimated in the generation of the public in our times.[2] In this chapter, I wish to elaborate on the thesis that the public sphere cannot unfold spontaneously, but needs specific conditions. In doing so, I wish to go beyond the claim that the public needs supportive institutions that help individuals to come together as a public whose main focus is deliberation on political issues. Instead, I wish to argue that public goods are particularly useful in providing material conditions for the generation and regeneration of the public.

The capacity of public goods to do so results from their characteristics. To call something a public good, the item has to fulfill two conditions: Access barriers have no selective effects, and a basic level is available to each person. In specifying the effects of common usage of public goods, it becomes obvious that public goods have positive side effects for societies in that they help build the public. In this chapter I shall explain how this process and the public are interconnected. In order to do that, I will also have to explain the underlying concept of the public. Furthermore, it has to be said that some public goods serve the public particularly well. The examples I shall discuss in this chapter are all from that subgroup of public goods. I shall call them *connectivity goods*.

My claim in this chapter is twofold. My *first* claim is that public goods are essential constituencies of the public. Public goods provide the specific conditions that a flourishing public needs. My *second* claim is that the reconsideration of the role of public goods for the public shows that the classic approach to the public sphere also needs specification. I shall demonstrate this consequence in discussing John Dewey's understanding of the public as presented in *The Public and Its Problems*[3] and Jürgen Habermas's conception of the public. The choice of these approaches is due to the impact both conceptions have on an understanding of the public sphere in political philosophy and beyond. They also represent two different approaches to the public that both connect to public goods.

The chapter is organized as follows: The *first section* explains the ways in which public goods help generate the public. I shall argue that public goods serve as a subtle layer which enables groups of individuals to self-identify as a public. The public-generating power of public goods can be derived from features that distinguish this group of goods. The main argument will be that due to their characteristics as goods whose benefits are to some degree available to each person and whose benefits can be chosen voluntarily, public goods are particularly suitable to support the genesis of the public. In the *second section*, the arguments will then be rendered more precise in that their scope and also their limitations will be explained. The *third section* embarks on the notion of the public that stems from John Dewey's elaboration on *The Public and Its Problems*.[4] Dewey's approach to the public is an analytic account. It takes into account the necessity to cope commonly with some particularly heavy externalities. It can be argued that Dewey anticipates the possibility of redefining public goods in terms of *public bads* and in terms of *negative externalities*. In doing so, he misses the important link between public goods and the public. I shall explain in which way public goods can provide the missing link. The *fourth section* of this chapter elaborates on the relationship of my analysis of the public to the well-known approach to the public that has been reasoned by Jürgen Habermas and echoed by Charles Taylor.[5] Their notion of the public can be considered as forming the opposite pole of a scale that defines the public. While Dewey's notion of the public is a minimal notion, Jürgen Habermas and Charles Taylor approach the public from its opposite angle. It is a rich and demanding concept. From the perspective of public goods theory, this theory can be rounded up by being given some foothold in the realm of public goods. The *fifth section* gives a summary of the arguments.

One further remark is necessary. I am well aware that it is a long road from the notion of public goods to the public sphere in the sense of the Enlightenment. In particular in Jürgen Habermas's writings Immanuel Kant's initial idea is still echoed, which implies that progress of a political society can best be expected under conditions of freedom of thought and rational exchange. The public forum is the community of citizens that succeeds in reasoning together without falling back into dogmatism and blind submission under political power. Public goods do not immediately enter that picture. But when one starts thinking about material conditions of the demanding reality of the public sphere, at some point, public goods come in. It is the aim of this chapter to give a theoretical assessment of that point.

THE ROLE OF PUBLIC GOODS IN GENERATING THE PUBLIC

In discussing the role of public goods, the first important step is a remainder of their peculiarity. According to the definition given in chapter one, goods are called public goods when they meet the conditions of open access and basic availability. These conditions say that access barriers do not have selective effects for the range of beneficiaries. And a public good is to some degree available to each person who wants to profit from it. This means that up to a certain degree—the basic level—they can be enjoyed by many users simultaneously without reducing the benefits that accrue to each user; furthermore, each person has access to them. The second step is a closer look at how the public sphere and public goods are related to each other. My hypothesis is that the importance of public goods has generally been underestimated. If public goods are present, they are taken for granted; if they have already started to vanish, consequences other than the loss of the public are more obvious because they are hurtful. Yet, one of the most striking effects remains unnoticed: If public goods perish, an essential precondition for a flourishing public is already lost.

I shall now argue that the public cannot unfold spontaneously. Instead, it needs specified conditions to unfold. These specified conditions can best be realized by public goods. For clarity of my argumentation, I set aside the question of which background institutions have to be presupposed for the continued existence of public goods. My focus will be on the relation between public goods and the public. I shall defend the claim that public goods contribute to generating the public. They do so by offering the occasion for qualitatively distinct experiences. In order to explain these qualities I distinguish between three different spheres of interaction between beneficiaries that are generated by public goods. These are: *spheres of mutual awareness*, *spheres of reliability*, and *spheres of experienced equality*. The existence of a public good helps stimulate these spheres which can be regarded as patterns of interactions in which mutual awareness, reliability, and equality can be experienced. These experiences do not presuppose existing patterns of exchange or communication; they rather also emerge between strangers. All three spheres shall now be introduced. After having presented the underlying ideas I shall discuss the reasons why public goods can be expected to have these effects.

Public goods are the realm of encounters between strangers. People come together and mingle in public places. Public places, national parks and landscape invite people of all kinds. And even though hospitals and educational institutions primarily fulfill other functions, they also provide places where people come together and get connected. Alluding to centers of interaction or of nodes in networks means speaking metaphorically. However, regarding public goods, these pictures are telling ones. Public goods provoke intersections between activities and consequences of actions of different people and the awareness of sharing a common realm. As Charles Taylor states: "Spaces of this kind become more and more important in modern urban society, where large numbers of people rub shoulders, unknown to each other, without dealing with each other, and yet affecting each other, forming the inescapable context of each other's lives."[6]

Although interactions nowadays do not necessarily take place in a real place in the form of a real exchange of views and words, we should not exaggerate our lifestyle and conceive of ourselves as cyber-entities. It might also be true that our interactions take more and more place in the sphere of the market, where we encounter each other as customers and trade-partners. Both developments—the encounters through electronic media and the encounter as participants in the market—do not diminish, but indeed stress the importance of experiences of accidental interaction which are stimulated by public goods. If no public parks, no public space in cities, no streets and sidewalks were available, people who are strangers to each other would rarely engage in the minimal interaction to share a common place, to exchange views, and perhaps also to engage in some more or less unimportant phrases about the weather.

The encounter between individual persons within a public space also provokes a distinct kind of awareness. In public places, people interact with each other and do so without a particular intent. Mutual awareness may not be as demanding as a recognition that goes beyond taking notice each other, but is important to building relations that support self-respect and self-esteem.[7] The experience of being part of and participating in mixed communities is not as demanding as taking into notice the personality of another individual and paying tribute to his or her particular wishes, aims, or qualities. But it is important because it provides a background for further steps in developing a public. In short, public goods provide *spheres of mutual awareness*.

Public goods also create *spheres of reliability*. Reliability already results from public goods being more complex and stable than other goods. If we woke up one day to find that the city playground, the streets, the schools, and the quality of the air had vanished or totally transformed over night, we would know that something very serious had happened. This is no situation we expect in our daily lives. Without the security that some goods are available and will be available, a subtle layer in our understanding of the world that provides us with a minimal amount of safety is missing. This aspect echoes and transcends the debate on "social trust" in recent contributions on civil society.[8] Yet, spheres of reliability go beyond that experience. When goods are accessible without further preconditions and when a basic level of availability has been guaranteed, individuals can be reassured that they do not have to worry about their access conditions. In this sense it can be argued that reliability is correlated more generally with public goods.

Finally, public goods create *spheres of experienced equality*. If events such as marathons, city festivals, sporting events, and public lectures are "public events," each citizen is invited to participate in them. In that respect, the events are like public goods. They also have antisegregation effects. I now wish to draw attention to the fact that such events do not only have that effect on the citizenry. They also contribute to the feeling of being part of the public. The underlying mechanism is the experience of effective equality. Goods that are public goods are—in the sense determined—freely accessible and equally available to each citizen. One of the effects is that each participant can make the experience that others receive the same offer to participate as oneself. This is more than mutual awareness alone. This awareness includes that the same chance to participate and the same level of benefits apply to each participant. It supports an understanding for being equal to each other person.

Interaction becomes a new quality because of this awareness. As for public goods, each person will participate according to the same access conditions, and this is something everyone will know. If the other person has the same opportunity to participate in a public good, she also knows that she will not have more or less privileges in this situation than I myself will enjoy. In discussing this effect of public goods I do not assume that each person is always aware of this effect. Experienced equality, however, is something that can be made explicit, and this is important for the self-understanding of members of the public. What is crucial is that we are speaking about an experience that stems from the reality of goods that are equally accessible to all.

To summarize the argument so far: Public goods sustain and stimulate distinct exchange patterns within a political community. These *spheres of mutual awareness*, *spheres of reliability*, and *spheres of experienced equality* are essential in that they help individuals to interpret themselves as connected with each other in a certain way. It is important to notice that these spheres may vary with the specific good at its center. Some goods provide particularly well-suited conditions for stimulating these spheres of interchange. Examples would be public transport, infrastructure in terms of telecommunication, public space, public parks and the Internet. These goods are particularly well suited to stimulate processes of mutual awareness. Yet, the emergence of these spheres exclusively depends on the general features of public goods.

Public goods do not cause or produce the public, but they stimulate it and contribute to its continued existence. In the remainder of this chapter, I first wish to challenge this argument and then discuss this proposal in relation to well-known theories of the public sphere that differ from this approach.

CHALLENGING THE ARGUMENTS

For arriving at a precise understanding of the arguments that have been given so far, it is necessary to get a clear view of their scope and limits. I shall pose the most challenging question first. It is the question of why private goods should not have the same effects as public goods and possibly even do better in terms of generating the public. Some authors claim that a market-style economy has democratizing effects in precisely that respect: no one is excluded from participation in processes of exchange and therefore also in the chance to ameliorate his or her own situation.[9] In addition, in the market place everyone is treated equally. It can be argued that for coordination between different, self-interested individuals, markets are better institutions than public goods regimes.

The first reply to this argument is that markets are limited to those who can participate in them. Markets do not necessarily include all citizens, nor can markets flourish unless some minimal conditions have been established beforehand: For having equalizing effects, the effective protections of private property and systems of law and order have to be established in advance. Even then, markets do not imply distributive principles that guarantee access and benefits for all. A minimal provision with capital of all participants would be another important precondition for the effect of markets to give anyone a chance.

Setting these aspects aside, the argument still hints at an important point: Even if it can be argued that compared to markets, public goods are inclusive, this does not imply that public goods cannot be *provided* by the private sector. It is important to notice that the arguments about public goods do not exclude that perspective on public goods. Instead, it can be argued that mixed regimes are more favorable in that they provide a reliable source of financial means and—additionally—can help to avoid "cultures of dependency."[10] Public-private partnerships, e.g., can help to support an engaged public.

Another important point is that—in reality—public goods do not appear as those peaceful spheres of interaction that were presented in my analysis. Frequently, devices of public transportation have been destroyed, public spaces have been used as favorable places for conflicts and clashes over conflicting interests, public parks have been places of crime. A first reply to this counterargument is that if all these things happen, something has already gone wrong. Maybe, communities have forgotten how to benefit from public goods; maybe there is no longer a minimal agreement about the worth of public goods.[11] A more sophisticated answer can point to the fact that a conflict over public goods is not detrimental, but normal. The important question is whether or not the conflict turns out to be constructive and contributes to the public sphere. At this point, it becomes clear that *the public* is not identical with *public goods*; nor is the existence of public goods sufficient for defining a *public forum*. More specified conditions of how the public can learn to deal with conflicting interests have to be elaborated. But it still can be argued that public goods provide a subtle layer from which a public can evolve.

A final challenge results from approaches to the public that do not wish to go beyond the sheer fact of association. Either individuals choose associations or they do not. This argument implies that it would be wrong to stimulate patterns of interaction and exchange by public goods. Answering this argument it can be said that it ignores the fact that individuals sometimes need support to make the first step. The idea that individuals sometimes choose retreat into the private realm does not necessarily say that individuals always prefer this kind of behavior. The debate on the adaptation of preferences demonstrates that individuals sometimes need experiences to reshape their preferences.[12] When individuals have a chance to participate in public goods and the issue of public goods is made a matter of common concern and debate, this may also change the individual's ideas about public goods.

JOHN DEWEY'S BEWILDERED PUBLIC

I shall now turn to the place of public goods within theories on the public. The first author I shall deal with is John Dewey. He presents a theory in which public goods do already play an important, though indirect, role. He argues that the public emerges when individuals become aware of severe negative side effects of collective action. They then understand the need to work collectively against these side effects. In this line of thought, an idea of public goods is already present. Yet, Dewey falls short of switching from public bads to public goods. In discussing Dewey I shall first discuss his approach and then add the missing perspective.

In his theory on the public, John Dewey defends a view that has been identified as a *functional definition* of the public. The emergence of the public depends on the view that problems with undesirable side effects of collective action cannot be resolved by individuals alone. Instead, society has to come together and try to resolve these problems collectively.

Yet, his analysis of the public can also be regarded as an assessment of the minimal conditions for the emergence of the public sphere. As a starting point, I shall introduce some of John Dewey's observations.[13] After having introduced Dewey's concerns about the public, I will turn to Dewey's analysis of the genesis of the public. In his discussion of the public, Dewey is aware of the problem of how the public can be generated. Yet, at one point he does not acknowledge the relation between the conditions for a flourishing public and the public correctly. Instead of focusing exclusively on negative externalities—as Dewey proposes—it is necessary to focus on goods that help stimulate the public. This thesis has to be explained in some detail.

Almost a century ago, John Dewey observed that "the Public seems to be lost; it is certainly bewildered."[14] His complaints concern corrupt and chaotic governments as well as misrepresentation of both the real concerns and the real desires of people. Dewey also comments on the effects of a wave of industrialization which did not only bring new devices of telecommunication and mass transportation, but also threatened to disrupt the bonds of community life. Dewey's analysis, however, does not aim merely at commenting these developments; rather he is interested in the influence on patterns of interaction and consequences of actions. The industrial revolution not only speeds up communication and mobilizes societies, but also brings about a situation of bewilderment for societies: But the machine age has so enormously expanded, multiplied, intensified and complicated the scope of the indirect consequences, have formed such immense and consolidated unions in action, on an impersonal rather than an community basis, that the resultant public cannot identify and distinguish itself."[15]

When individuals and private actors start to act, chains of consequences are set in motion that reach beyond the circle of actors and can inflict harm on others. In Dewey's view, the awareness of these qualitatively and quantitatively outstanding consequences gives birth to the public.[16] It is crucial for understanding Dewey's view of the public that it relies on the categories of practices and of consequences. Actions have causal consequences and the criss-crossing chains sometimes result in lasting, extensive, and serious effects. People are interested in solving these conflicts. Political institutions have to serve the interests of people in precisely these respects. This does not entail that all kinds of effects have to be considered. Only if non-desirable, severe and extensive consequences surface, people become aware of them, and the common interests aims at avoiding and reducing these side effects. In short, "Indirect, extensive, enduring, and serious consequences of conjoint and interacting behavior call a public into existence having a common interest in controlling these consequences."[17] The idea of a functional role of political institutions does not amount to a political theory at this point. Rather, the more modest goal is to present an explanation for the emergence of the public and the need for political institutions. The rules of law are considered as forceful devices for effectively sanctioning and forbidding activities whose consequences are against the common interest. "Rules of law are in fact the institution of conditions under which persons make their arrangements with one another. They are structures that canalize action; they are active forces only as are banks that confine the flow of a stream, and are commands only in the sense in which the banks command the current."[18]

At this point, the similarity between Dewey's proposal and the treatment of public goods in politics today becomes particularly apparent. It is common practice to discuss public goods, particularly environmental goods such as clean air and water, in terms of negative externalities.[19] If a private firm pollutes the air, this has a negative impact on those who wish to breathe clean air. Processes of industrial production produce unintentional negative side effects. Once these negative externalities have been identified, devices are necessary to enforce either their reduction or at least a compensation for those suffering from them.[20] To be sure, focusing on externalities and forcing the actors responsible for negative externalities to internalize these effects is an effective and necessary device in public goods politics.[21] It is, however, not sufficient in terms of generating the public.

The *first* reason is that there is a systematic problem that Dewey cannot solve. It is hard to define negative externalities beyond obvious examples without defining what the good, which should be protected, actually is. In many cases, Dewey's reliance on "severe" and "long-lasting" consequences will be too imprecise. For such a definition, some ideas about the endangered goods have to be introduced. If the air is polluted and water not clean, it is one thing to hold someone accountable and to force a firm to internalize negative side effects of their activities. It is another thing to define negative side effects in the first place. To rely on complaints of individuals who feel disturbed will not solve the problem—at least not unless they can supplement their desires by appealing to some kind of entitlement to clean air and water. To show that some basic goods are good for all citizens is at least in pragmatic terms the easier way to go.

The *second* reason why Dewey's concept is not perfectly convincing is that he does not take into account that in some cases a stimulus to connect with each other does have to be presupposed. In Dewey's account, the most important link between interactions and the public are what we call today negative externalities or undesired spillover effects. Negative externalities can be interpreted as public bads. Yet, the recognition of public bads does not have the same effects as the awareness and real experience of public goods. As goods with overall fair access conditions, public goods help citizens to connect with each other. Dewey, instead, does not take into account any centers that could help the public emerge from the chaotic realm of interactions between individuals. It can also be argued that the more rapidly the environment and social world changes, the more necessary those centers are for citizens to understand themselves as part of a more comprehensive citizenry.

These insights can be translated in Dewey's terminology. Dewey is aware of something he calls "recognition" of the public. Dewey is worried about a "loss of the public." According to his view, the diagnosed loss of the public results from a whole bundle of different factors and developments. Modern lifestyle implies an increase in terms of mobility; face-to-face communities lose their meaning. These factors might be important; yet, Dewey does not take into account a transformation of communal life into modern forms of the public. Instead, he recalls some different cures.

Among the factors that contribute to the loss of the public, the lack of sufficient scientific knowledge is considered a major one. As Dewey explicitly states: "An inchoate public is capable of organization only when indirect consequences are perceived, and when it is possible to project agencies that order their occurrence. At present, many consequences are felt rather than perceived; they are suffered, but they cannot be said to be known, for they are not, by those who experience them, referred to their origins."[22] If Dewey was right, how can it be that the public today is still bewildered and seems to be lost, although we have a much better understanding of the origins of pollution, the death of certain species and the deterioration of all kinds of environmental treasures? Never before has scientific progress yielded a more profound understanding of externalities and spillover effects than today. The knowledge in natural sciences and in game theory, the technical means for computation of data, and the simulation of consequences have been developing rapidly; telecommunication devices have never been better; even regulatory agencies have never been as elaborate as today, regulation has been made a matter of prior concern in all developed countries.

In my view, Dewey did not detect the main factor for the loss of the public. Negative externalities are not a good folio for societies to identify with. Instead, the presence of public goods generates structures that support the genesis and the flourishing of the public. Public goods can underpin what Dewey calls a form of self-awareness of the public and self-recognition as a public.

AN EXTENSION OF HABERMAS'S PUBLIC FORUM

Now I shall turn to a concept of the public sphere that—in contrast to Dewey's minimal definition—can be called a maximum definition of the public. The definition stems from Habermas's theory on democracy and has had a major impact on theories on deliberative democracy.[23] The approaches on democracy that acknowledge the essential role of the public for democratic performances do not necessarily endorse a concept of deliberation and reasoning which is as strong a concept as the one in Habermas's Kantian republicanism. But for Habermas, democracy without an active and reasoning public is inconceivable.[24] He connects this view with a moral point of view: Legitimacy of democratic practices stems from reasonable acceptance from all citizens.

The sphere of life in which political democracy is rooted is the public. In reasoning on matters of common concern, the public unfolds what Habermas calls political power. Yet, it is not this effect that Habermas is primarily interested in. Instead, the most striking aspect of the theory is the presupposition that individuals enter a communicative process under preconditions that they cannot choose. In his transcendental analysis of the background conditions of free and rational exchange, Habermas demonstrates that individuals already enter this situation of common deliberation and communication with a set of expectations that, although they are not made explicit, shape this process. In particular, individuals presuppose that the other person will tell the truth and that she will try to give the best possible judgment in normative terms. When reasoning over a normative claim, this leads to a situation in which each person tries to understand the position of each participant and they collectively try to find the best arguments. As a result from that procedure, rational agreement can be reached and the best possible solution will be found.

This ethical approach translates into a political theory which takes the role of public deliberation seriously.[25] As a technique with which collective problems can best be discussed and resolved, Habermas's proposal includes the idea that the Parliament has to be reshaped accordingly. Yet, Habermas also stresses the importance of a societal realm in which that practice can best be played out. In his approach, it is the public form that offers room for communicative action. To summarize Habermas's account four essential characteristics of the public can be listed:

Following Habermas, the public is constituted by four essential characteristics:

1. The public is constituted by processes of rational deliberation about issues of common concern.

2. The public unfolds as rather self-standing, nevertheless interconnected subspheres to which all citizens have access.[26]
3. The public aims at gaining political influence. Although it is itself not part of the established political system, it is concerned with gaining influence on politically managed matters of common concern beyond participation through official polls.
4. The public is supported and strengthened by networks of voluntary associations.[27]

According to this account, the public is a distinctive sphere that is embedded in the broader realm of civil society with its various voluntary associations and social actors.[28] At the core of the public lies a rational and argumentative exchange about matters of common interest. In a democratic state, each person can participate in this common deliberation which is promoted and facilitated by print media, broadcasting, and, recently, the Internet.

In relating these ideas to public goods, I do *not* wish to criticize the idea that public deliberation is essential for the existence of a public forum. I also do *not* want to call into question that a vital public sphere is necessary for granting the legitimacy of political decisions. In confronting Habermas's account with public goods I rather wish to question the additional features that round up his theoretical background in *Between Facts and Norms*. In particular, I wish to elaborate on three critiques that result from a public goods approach to the public. The *first critique* relates to the role of associations in contrast to the role of public goods, the *second* places emphasis on the material basis of the public, the *third* discusses the claim for independence of the public as opposed to its need for support by public goods.

My *first critique* relates to the alleged role of associations. In elaborating on the relation between the concept of legitimacy and the role of the public, Habermas places emphasis on the role of associations. They connect the public forum with the level of private life. Yet, one may doubt whether or not associations can really provide the social interconnection the public needs as its supplement and precondition. Associations focus on special goals and attract individuals with common interests. Public goods, instead, appear to be much more suitable to create mixed communities and to support mutual awareness not only among citizens but also among different groups within societies. As goods whose entrance barriers do not have selective effects and as goods which are to some degree available to each citizen, public goods provide a more reliable focus not only for shared attention but also for interaction. This does not mean that the wider realm of civil society is not an important part of the public. The only thing I wish to say is that the role of voluntary associations differs from the role of public goods. When compared with each other, the role of voluntary associations loses its central meaning. While voluntary associations bundle forces and interests for shaping matters of common concern effectively, public goods provide a basic texture without which the public cannot flourish.

Secondly, one consequence of focusing on the exchange of rational arguments between free and equal persons as a realization of the public is a reductive notion of the public. And this, too, seems counterintuitive. The public is the medium in which citizens can move, can meet each other and can experience themselves as citizens. Habermas and authors who follow Habermas might be right that deliberation about matters of common concern is the most important factor in forming a public that is strong enough to build up—what Habermas calls—political power.[29] But the public is much broader than that. This becomes particularly apparent when the conditions of the formation of the public are taken into account. Even though the freedom and equality of citizens might find its most distinguished expression in public deliberation, it has a material side. Citizens also need to experience equality and need to be free to benefit from shared goods in order to create a kind of social glue and in order to enter reasonable debates with each other. Without the idea of equality in the material sense and without spheres of reliability, public deliberation misses its material roots.

Although I shall acknowledge the "metatopical" quality of the public in that the public makes use of modern information technology, my proposal includes two deviations from the deliberative approach. The *first* one is that the public cannot be completely separated from real experiences. The experience of distinct spheres, which I have just described are necessary for the continued existence of the public. The *second* modification relates to the particularity of public goods. Besides their functions in terms of connecting individuals with each other and providing spheres of reliability and spheres of experienced equality, they can also provide centers of common concern and thereby stimulate subspheres of the public. I shall turn to the precise relation between public goods and political decisions in chapters five and six. At this point, it suffices to acknowledge that the public is not as chaotic as Habermas presupposes. The subspheres of the public unfold around distinct experiences and on different scales. Public goods succeed in building centers for the public and they generate levels of the public from the local up to the global.[30] Having said all this, the conclusion is *not* that the public forum that Habermas envisions is not at the core of the processes forming a political will. But it can be argued that deliberation is "the crown" of the public rather than its core.

The *third point* I wish to consider with respect to the public is the need for a way of balancing the public's need for support by political institutions, on the one hand, and its independence, on the other. At first sight, introducing public goods appears to endanger the independence of the public that has been stressed by Habermas and his followers. My proposal regarding the public-generating power of public goods implies that instead of denying this need, it is more fruitful to make it explicit.

As a matter of fact, states are more and more interventionist in their practices. But the effects of interventionist practices accrue to voluntary associations as well as to public goods. State institutions model the realm of civil society by providing tax exemptions, by subsidizing one social actor and not another and so forth.[31] State practices reach deep into the realm of society. Instead of accepting a hidden agenda, the importance of some goods for the formation of the public should be accepted and the need for political support should openly be discussed. The public is the autonomous sphere of individuals with individual ideas and yet with a shared self-understanding as members of the public. Its existence ultimately depends on what individuals make of it and what they are ready to contribute to it. Whether or not public goods diminish the quality of the public as a self-standing sphere within society depends on how they are organized, but not on their qualities as public goods. I shall turn to this point in chapter five in more detail.

To summarize the argument, I wish to reconsider the four aspects of the original concept of the public and how they should be modified when public goods have been taken into account.

As for the focus on deliberation (1), the capacity to deliberate about issues of common concern is still an important part of the public sphere. The public is, however, entrenched in experienced equality and reliability. Without the reality of these dimensions, it is not likely that the public will ever reach the point of Habermasian deliberation.

As for the metatopical realization of the public (2), it is true that the public unfolds a dynamic that is not restricted to local meetings. It is, however, more realistic to conceive of the free unfolding of the public as still dependent on distinct experiences that go beyond experiences of rational exchange. Experiences of mutual awareness, of reliability, and of experienced equality that materialize around concrete public goods are necessary to reassure individuals that they are part of a larger public. People need chances for materialized reassurance. Public goods can provide people with the real experiences they need for actively participating in and understanding themselves as part of the public.

With respect to political influence (3), public goods can provide the grounds for individuals being willing to engage for common interests. Public goods nourish the hope and the prospect that equality, reliability, and real commitment are not mere fictions but rather part of daily reality. As for the drive toward political change, public goods not only support the generation of the public sphere. They might also offer a focus of concern for the citizenry. They thereby help to structure the efforts of the public.

As for the role of associations (4), I have indicated that I am skeptical regarding the forcefulness of voluntary associations in that they generate close social bonds and dense communities. Voluntary associations are a critical ingredient in civil society. But they alone cannot provide the ground on which a self-confident and still critical public can flourish. It can be added that some of the public functions that are generally attributed to associations can be better fulfilled by public goods: Public goods stimulate trust between strangers, provide the realm for diversity and mixed communities, and they might also provoke commitments and debates. Associations fulfill a different, but equally important function. They bring people together and help them to reinforce themselves in their shared interests and for building up political forms of power.[32]

BEYOND THE FACT OF ASSOCIATION

It is a major flaw of deliberative and liberal democracy not to understand the self-referential structure of the public. Although the existence of the public is most important in that it is an essential ingredient in democracies, this should not lead to reducing the analysis of the public to its unique function in democracy. The public can only flourish under conditions that cannot fully be captured in the language of basic rights and the guarantee of basic freedoms. Instead, the paradoxical claim for governments to establish conditions that limit their own power must reach the level of material goods. I have argued that public goods provide conditions for a public being in a situation to continuously regenerate itself.

In particular, due to their function as *connectivity goods* public goods add the crucial link that is missing in Dewey's analysis. According to Dewey's view, "There is no mystery about the fact of association, of an interconnected action which affects the activity of singular elements. There is no sense in asking how individuals come to be associated. They exist and operate in association. . . . There is, however, an intelligible question about human association—not the question how individuals or singular beings come to be connected, but how they come to be connected in just those ways which give human communities traits so different from those which mark assemblies of electrons, unions of trees in forests, swarms of insects, herds of sheep, and constellations of stars."[33] One of the main differences between Dewey's vision of the public and the proposal outlined in this chapter is that individuals can only form a public if they have reliable sources for the self-identification as a public.

One further thought can be added. That awareness cannot grow if societies and their political institutions are preoccupied with controlling the negative, accumulated side effects of human actions. To recognize itself, the public needs the centers of reliability and experienced equality that come with the provision of public goods. The public might be overtaxed without this backbone.

NOTES

1. Jürgen Habermas, *The Structural Transformation of the Public Sphere: An Inquiry into a Category of Bourgeois Society* (transl. Thomas Burger with

the assistance of Frederick Lawrence. Cambridge, UK: Polity Press, 1989); Michael Warner, *The Letters of the Republic: Publication and the Public Sphere in Eighteenth-Century America* (Cambridge, MA, and London, England: Harvard University Press, 1990).

2. Cass R. Sunstein, *republic.com* (Princeton and Oxford: Princeton University Press, 2002).

3. John Dewey, *The Public and Its Problems* (Athens: Swallow Press and Ohio University Press, 1954).

4. Dewey, *The Public.*

5. *See* Charles Taylor, *Modern Social Imaginaries* (Durham and London: Duke University Press, 2004), 83–99. Taylor explains the characteristics of the public sphere as a "metatopical realm" that spreads beyond its instantiation in real dialogues and political discussions.

6. Charles Taylor, *Varieties of Religion Today: William James Revisited* (Cambridge, MA, and London, UK: Harvard University Press, 2002), 86. Taylor calls common goods like parks "spaces of mutual display" which, against the backdrop of growing tendencies toward individualism, "seem to point to a new way of being together in society." Taylor, *Varieties of Religion*, 88. In the view defended in this chapter, Taylor's example presents one facet of subtle layers of the public that are supported by the availability of public goods.

7. In this respect, I agree with Nancy Rosenblum who reminds us that a politics of recognition is a demanding and maybe too demanding project for everyday life: "By definition, the politics of recognition seeks to alter the behavior of others. It looks for specific attestations of appreciation, or deference. Not content with 'easy spontaneity,' it forces people's hands and demands substantive acknowledgment of one's own sense of standing. Carried over into everyday interactions, recognition is liable to be impracticable in any case. For one thing, because it is so demanding. It requires considerable self-discipline to avoid specific action or gestures that group members regard as a slight or say will diminish their self-respect, and to adjust or demeanour and conduct to what counts for them as an adequate demonstration of regard." Nancy L. Rosenblum, *Membership & Morals: The Personal Uses of Pluralism in America* (Princeton, NJ: Princeton University Press, 1998), 355. Rosenblum also explains that people do not always want to be regarded as members of groups, but rather willfully throw off their ascriptive connections when moving around in the public sphere. *See* Rosenblum, *Membership*, 356. This is another argument for not overloading the public sphere with demanding ideas such as self-esteem, recognition or even community. It is necessary to find a middle level between too modest a conception that exclusively relies on regulating conflicts between individuals and a too demanding version which draws on ideals and bonds between individuals that do not accord with an understanding of individualism and freedom in the public sphere which characterizes a modern way of being.

8. For arguments why political communities depend on trust *see* Francis Fukuyama, "Trust: The Social Virtues and the Creation of Prosperity," in *The Essential Civil Society Reader: The Classic Essays*, ed. Don E. Eberly (Lanham et al.: Rowman and Littlefield, 2000), 257–266.

9. For a critical discussion of the argument that economic development supports democratization on a global level *see* Jadish Baghwati, *In Defense of Globalization* (New York: Oxford University Press, 2004), esp. chapter II.8.: "Democracy at Bay?," 92–105. Baghwati defends the view that economic development spurs democratization against the arguments that globalization rather constrains democratization either through anti-democratic countermovements or through the constraints it imposes on social spending.

10. For the over dependence on the welfare state from the perspective of collective-choice theory *see* Arthur Seldon, "Public Choice in Britain," in *Government Failure: A Primer in Public Choice*, ed. Gordon Tullock, Arthur Seldon, and Gordon L. Brady (Washington, DC: Cato Institute, 2002), 143–154.

11. For a discussion of city parks that suffer from neglect of the surrounding communities *see* Jane Jacobs, *The Death and Life of Great American Cities* (New York: Vintage Books, 1992), 95.

12. On "adaptive preferences" *see* Martha C. Nussbaum, *Women and Human Development: The Capabilities Approach* (Cambridge, UK: Cambridge University Press., 2000), 111–166.

13. John Dewey's conception of the public is a good starting point for elaborating on public goods and their impact on societies for another reason as well. He does not start with political institutions and an already set-up public, but with individuals in a pre-political sphere and their interactions. The adequate range of institutions can only be defined with reference to their function to solve conflicts between individuals. Hence, the analysis of what the conflicts over them are is prior. For this see John Dewey, *The Public*, 28–30.

14. Dewey, *The Public*, 116. My discussion of Dewey is focused on this text. To select this contribution results from the fact that it is Dewey's "only formal work of political philosophy" as Robert B. Westbrook notes in his elaborations on Dewey's political philosophy in: *John Dewey and American Democracy* (Ithaca and London: Cornell University Press, 1991), 300. Westbrook's distinction of several phases in the development of Dewey's philosophy shows that this late work of Dewey differs from his early political philosophy that was influenced by a Hegelian understanding of societies as organisms with qualitatively distinct spheres.

15. Dewey, *The Public*, 126.

16. Dewey, *The Public*, 47.

17. Dewey, *The Public*, 126.

18. Dewey, *The Public*, 54.

19. In giving this assessment, I do not deny that parts of the public goods problem can be translated into a theory of externalities. My point is rather, that this translation is not a comprehensive one, as theories relying on externalities tend to assume. If so, the authors also speak of public bads. For a critical survey over the link between public goods problems and externalities in economics *see* Richard Cornes and Todd Sandler, *The Theories of Externalities, Public Goods, and Club Goods* (Cambridge et al.: Cambridge University Press, 1986).

20. A well-known solution for solving these conflicts is presented by Roland Coase in his Coase theorem that is explained in "The Problem of Social Cost," *Journal of Law and Economics*, no. 3 (1960): 1–44. Coase interprets the conflict as a two-party conflict: Both the polluter and the actor being harmed by pollution have to get into a legal contract over an adequate solution for the conflict. Coase argues that if property rights have been defined comprehensively, solutions can easily be worked out and enforced. To the manifold critique this theorem has encountered, the logic of the "loss of the public" adds the point that even if Coase's solution was a practicable one, it could not provide the common centers of concern that are necessary for the evolution of a public.

21. This approach is used for elaborating international treaties to reduce air-pollution. For an example *see* Scott Barrett, "Montreal versus Kyoto: International Cooperation and the Global Environment," in *Global Public Goods: International Cooperation in the 21st Century*, ed. Inge Kaul, Isabelle Grunberg, and Marc A. Stern (New York and Oxford: Oxford University Press, 1999), 192–219.

22. Dewey, *The Public*, 131.

23. The concept of the public that has been elaborated by Jürgen Habermas and still stimulates debates over deliberative democracy goes back to his Habilitation: *Habermas The Structural Transformation* (Transl. Thomas Burger with the assistance of Frederick Lawrence, Cambridge: Polity, 1989). In this book, Habermas elaborates on the evolvement of the public as a distinct sphere in 18th-century Germany and Europe. Deliberation that aims at elaborating a reasonable consensus and deals with matters of common concern is not only distinguished by its independence from state institution and the private sphere, but also by necessary presuppositions that are implicit in the acts of communication. As truth-oriented speakers, the participants in deliberation offer reliabilities as for their later activities. The burden of proof for having come to the best possible agreement is that its consequences can voluntarily be accepted by all participants.

24. For the characterization of his position as Kantian Republicanism, *see* Jürgen Habermas, "'Reasonable' versus 'True,' or the Morality of Worldviews,"

in *The Inclusion of the Other: Studies in Political Philosophy*, ed. C. Cronin and P. De Greiff (Cambridge, MA: MIT Press, 1998), 92–93 and 101.

25. *See* Jürgen Habermas, *Between Facts and Norms: Contributions to a Discourse Theory of Law and Democracy* (Cambridge, MA: MIT Press, 1996).

26. For this characteristic trait of the public that is reinforced through new telecommunicative devices, Taylor has coined the term "metatopical spheres." *See* Taylor, *Modern Social Imaginaries*, 86. In Taylor's view, different from real assemblies "the public sphere . . . transcends such topical spaces. We might say that it knits together a plurality of such spaces into one larger space of nonassembly. The same public discussion is deemed to pass through our debate today, and someone else's earnest conversation tomorrow, and the newspaper interview Thursday, and so on. I call this larger kind of non-local common space 'metatopical.' The public sphere that emerges in the eighteenth century is a metatopical common space." Taylor, *Modern Social Imaginaries*, 86.

27. This fourth aspect can be regarded as a supplement of Habermas's original conception. To regard it as a necessary supplement certainly results from a growing awareness of the importance of civil society. It is not possible at this point to embark on the concept of civil society; for the importance of political society being embedded in the wider field of civil society *see* Mark E. Warren, *Democracy and Association* (Princeton and Oxford: Princeton University Press, 2001), 35 and 77–78.

28. Note that this account—even though the legitimatory role of the public is not explicitly addressed in my discussion—covers the models of the public in deliberative democracy and in liberal democracy as characterized by Seyla Benhabib in "Models of the Public Space: Hannah Arendt, the Liberal Tradition and Jürgen Habermas," in *Habermas and the Public Sphere*, ed. Craig Calhoun (Cambridge, MA: MIT Press, 1991), 73–98.

29. Michael Warner portrays the role of the evolvement of the print media in the United States. His study can be paralleled to Habermas's discussion of the emergence of the public in Europe. *See* Warner, *The Letters of the Republic*.

30. A variety of examples is discussed in: Inge Kaul, Isabelle Grunberg, and Marc A. Stern, eds., *Global Public Goods: International Cooperation in the 21st Century* (New York and Oxford: Oxford University Press, 1999).

31. Mark E. Warren criticizes that Tocqueville's associational model of civil society does not take into account this point. According to Warren, it neglects nongovernmental forms of power as well as the influence of states on the associational sphere. As for the United States, Warren notices that more and more associations are endowed with state-like regulatory functions as well as increasingly subsidized by public finance. This political influence is not necessarily impartial

and it might violate claims for neutrality of state practices. "Government attention to particular policy areas produces a 'crowd in' effect, increasing the numbers of associations and their activities." Warren, *Democracy and Association*, 33. According to Warren, the Tocquevillian approach "obscures the ways in which so much associational life today is intertwined with the powers and resources of governments" (Warren, *Democracy and Association*, 33) and neither can nor does take into account the interventionist practices of welfare-oriented states.

32. Much emphasis is given to the impact of associations in providing necessary training of civic virtues and in strengthening democracy. For a recent overview over the debate on the role of voluntary associations see the contributions in Amy Gutmann, ed., *Freedom of Association* (Princeton, NJ: Princeton University Press, 1998).

33. Dewey, *The Public*, 23–24.

5

CLAIMS FOR SOCIAL JUSTICE

Societies are complex systems that produce and distribute social and economic goods. This approach to political communities, famously theorized by John Rawls and his successors, has sharpened the view on problems of social justice. According to this view, the production and distribution of goods goes well beyond the sphere of industrial life. As for social justice, freedom, access to privileged positions and even self-esteem figure as primary goods whose fair distribution is at stake.[1] Although Rawls is a vigorous defender of distribution and the distributive paradigm, he also argues that political institutions should refrain from supporting what in his view have to remain the objects of voluntary associations. In *A Theory of Justice,* Rawls states that "the principles of justice do not permit subsidizing universities and institutes, or opera and the theater, on the grounds that these institutions are intrinsically valuable, and that those who engage in them are to be supported even at some significant expense to others who do not receive compensating benefits. Taxation for these purposes can be justified only as promoting directly or indirectly the social conditions that secure the equal liberties and as advancing in an appropriate way the long-term interests of the least advantaged."[2]

Rawls is right in claiming that politics must be impartial. Less clear, however, is whether Rawls is also right in claiming that taxes should only be used as a means of redistribution in favor of the least advantaged members of society. This does not only limit the range of welfare goods that can be supported by the political community. It also has the effect that states cannot engage in providing a variety of public goods. In this chapter, I shall argue that a list of public goods actually serves the realization of social justice within society. When tax payments are needed to realize this agenda, it is also justified to finance public goods by means of public finance. Yet, to understand the link between public goods and claims of social justice, we need to develop a theoretical approach which goes beyond the idea of fair distribution of goods and bads. Instead, I shall argue for an approach to social justice that can be summarized as favoring social inclusion.

My argumentation falls into six sections. In *section one*, I will present the idea that social justice can be spelled out in terms of social inclusion. Claims for social justice and their realization will be interpreted as demands for non-exclusive goods and their progressive fulfillment. In *section two*, I shall discuss several ways of introducing public goods into the debate on social justice. This includes a discussion of some critical distinctions in theories on social justice and a discussion of the "currency problem." In *section three*, I shall defend a principle of fairness. It says that it is unfair *not* to provide public goods when three conditions are met: These goods belong to a group of goods that are particularly necessary for people to develop a basically good life; they are part of a shared story of societal progress; and provision as a public good does not result in burdens for a society that cannot be carried.

In *section four*, I shall go deeper into the discussion of the first condition. In defending the view that some public goods serve a basically good life, I wish to rely on Martha Nussbaum's capabilities approach. She argues that political institutions should provide citizens with a basic level of goods that they need to develop "central human functional capabilities."[3] These capabilities, in turn, are preconditions for realizing a basically good life. In discussing the scope of the argument for public goods, it becomes clear that the capabilities approach is useful in giving an idea of a list of goods that meet the public goods conditions and are simultaneously related to demands of justice. This is the level of evidence that public goods theory needs. In *section five*, I shall defend the claim that that principle is adequate in defending the core meaning of social justice. In some respects it even trumps the distributive paradigm that dominates the discourse on social justice in political philosophy. *Section six* provides a perspective on public goods as social equalizers.

SOCIAL JUSTICE AS SOCIAL INCLUSION

Asked about social justice, it is likely that one would start with explaining egalitarian ideals. This would imply ideas about the enhancement of equal opportunities or the achievement of an equal basic standard of welfare. It would probably also include equal conditions of freedom of all citizens. The story of social justice, however, could also be interpreted in a different way.[4] Social justice can also be conceived of as the transition toward a situation in which public goods are available. Under that description, social justice still has to do with egalitarian ideals. One defining feature of public goods is that they are to some degree available to each person who wishes to profit from them (basic availability condition). Yet, the other defining feature can also be expressed in terms of social justice. According to the open access condition, no one who actually wants to profit from a public good will be excluded from doing so. Public goods have non-segregation effects. And these effects are critical to a story of justice that explains social justice in terms of social inclusion.

In order to illustrate this point, it is helpful to reconsider the rise of the welfare state. One crucial point for the rise of social justice can be seen in the aftermath of the industrial revolution. Industrialization not only led to a mass production of private goods but also to mass impoverishment. In this situation, the building of institutions that could forcefully fight poverty and desperation was a politically innovative idea. The state supported institutions that could provide the means that were necessary for effectively fighting social injustice in mass societies. Insurance systems that guaranteed a minimal provision in the case of a desperate situation were something like a beginning. Initially, they were available only to those involved in the working process.[5] Today, in many regions of the world each person has access to them. The important transition in terms of social justice is the guaranteed access to a set of goods that must be available to each person in desperate situations. Yet, this process is accompanied by another development. The transition in terms of social justice also includes the step from exclusive goods to goods that each citizen has access to. The amelioration in terms of social justice is not limited to the availability of a safety net. Social justice also finds its realizations in terms of a growing level of availability of the goods mentioned.

Another, very different perspective on the development of modern societies can explain the same idea from a different point of view. At the end of the 18th century, pieces of art were torn loose from the court and the church in Europe. Until then, arts were reserved to the realm of cultus in the church or to the court where artists were given order to portray members of the court. The autonomy of pieces of art that materialized in building museums was the decisive step to open pieces of art to the public. Music was also strictly related to religious events and to the court. As late as the beginning of the nineteenth century, private concerts were supplemented by public concerts. Even though this does not contribute to social justice in the literal sense, equal access to cultural goods can be considered as a major step towards a community of citizens that regard themselves as equal.

Thomas Nipperdey, a historian, interprets the transformation from private to public goods as closely related to the rise of a citizenry in the modern sense of the word.[6] This process was not reserved to the elite among citizens, the "Bildungsbürgertum." Instead, the new interrelatedness between the daily life and citizens and culture reached all sections. When Beethoven died in 1827, all pupils had a day off; twenty- to thirty-thousand people followed his coffin.[7] The rise of a self-confident citizenry was accompanied by a process that can be described as a transformation of private goods into public ones.

The most obvious examples of how social justice materializes in terms of public goods relate to situations when unfair access barriers to common goods are removed. The bus boycott in Montgomery, Alabama, is remembered as one of the most sustained and coordinated efforts in the history of the civil rights movement. Courageous individuals like Mrs. Rosa Parks succeeded in fighting a situation in which equal access to buses was denied to black persons. Before, black persons had to take a seat in a special section and were forced to give up their seat when the bus was overcrowded. The bus company in Montgomery did not hire black drivers; drivers often insulted and demeaned black passengers. Through many boycotts of buses, black activists—among them the famous Martin Luther King—and ordinary persons step by step succeeded in ending the situation of segregation. On November 13, 1956, the Supreme Court ruled that the city ordinances concerning seating on the buses violated the Fourteenth Amendment. The Supreme Court ruled that discriminatory rules had to stop.[8]

These examples describe very different events and developments.[9] Yet, in all three examples, something would be missing if social justice were exclusively interpreted in terms of welfare goods and in terms of distributing them according to rules of fairness. Instead, social justice also means the idea that a range of goods is no longer reserved to a special group of individuals. Thus, each person who wishes to profit from that good meets access barriers that allow her to do so. In addition, competition does not hinder her from doing so as long as there is a basic level of provision. This intuitively plausible idea has to be rendered more precise and shall be defended in the remainder of this chapter.

PUBLIC GOODS IN THEORIES OF SOCIAL JUSTICE

For introducing public goods into the debate on social justice, the first thing to notice is that public goods differ from goods that are usually at the center of these theories. In discussing goods, two alternatives present themselves. On the one hand, one might turn to goods as "overall useful means" for individuals in developing a life plan and in realizing a good life. Even though John Rawls fills that category with a bundle of different goods—a system of liberties, economic means, chances on good positions, and self-esteem—the basic idea of a good is that of a useful instrument in realizing things that are valuable.[10] Ultimately, this implication is derived from the concept of private goods that individuals purchase in favour of doing things they like to do. On the other hand, the meaning of a good implies that it is regarded as a valuable object. In this second sense of the word, the value that accrues to the good might either be attributed as a personal judgment or it might result from a shared perspective on that item. In political philosophy, the second meaning of the word "good" is particularly important. An example is provided in Michael Walzer's theory of justice.[11]

The concept of a public good differs from both. Public goods are not called goods because they are useful means in realizing the two moral capacities of persons, namely a sense of justice and the capacity of having a life plan, nor are they built on the common bonds that communities can offer. Public goods are rather called goods in the first place because they offer a range of benefits to individuals. Moreover, they deserve the name public goods when they serve democratic societies in some important respects. At first glance, public goods do not fit into the debate on social justice.

Yet, two options to reintroduce public goods into the debate on social justice can be elaborated when two theoretical challenges are taken seriously. Even though theories on social justice cover a vast field, two central problems can roughly be summarized as the debate about the *currency of justice* and as the debate about the alleged *universalism of claims for justice*. I shall explain both problems in turn in order to be in a position to explain how they help to discuss public goods as related to claims of social justice.

Even though authors unanimously agree that justice cannot be explained without reference to an idea of equality, they disagree about the adequate standard for measuring equality. This question has been labelled the "currency problem."[12] The widest gap opens between *resourcists* on the one hand and *welfarists* on the other. The former argue that individuals should get access to an equal set of resources. That view is motivated by the insight that the state should distribute particularly important goods according to standards of equality without intermingling with preferences and choices of individuals.[13] Welfarists, instead, argue that in the end the achievement of a situation of experienced welfare counts. This view presupposes the possibility of interpersonal comparisons of welfare. If preference satisfaction is the chosen standard of comparison, it is also necessary to show that preferences and their satisfaction can in some way be quantified.[14]

The currency problem is of particular importance regarding public goods regimes. If there weren't a third possibility of spelling out the problem of social justice, there would be no chance to relate issues concerning public goods with issues of social justice. The reason for this disconnectedness is the fact that access to public goods can neither be defined exclusively in terms of resources nor in terms of achievements. As for the first alternative, the resource approach, to profit from public goods might be helpful in realizing a life plan. However, public goods are not resources in the sense of items that allow for multiple uses. They are not overall useful means to realize a good life, either. Instead, the benefits one can derive from them are correlated with the specific good. As for the possibility of a welfarist account, public goods cannot directly be related to outcomes either.

Because of these difficulties, the availability of an alternative is mandatory for public goods theory. Fortunately, Amartya Sen and Martha C. Nussbaum have made the proposal of something like a "third way." Instead of relying exclusively on resources or on personal achievements, social justice relates to resources that provide the basis for the very possibility of achievements.[15] I shall shortly come to that approach in more detail and explain why it is suited for an account on social justice regarding public goods. So, I need to explain the second theoretical challenge: the decision for either a universalistic or a particularistic approach.

As for the universalism problem, debates focus on whether or not principles of justice can be justified without being limited to specific situations or persons. *Universalists* hold the view that claims for justice can be defended in a way that the answers given apply to each situation. In that sense, claims of justice are universal claims. *Particularists*, instead, hold the view that ideas about social justice can only be defended in relation to specific situations and specified claims. In particular, there are no universal principles.

Reasons for both positions differ. One way to defend universalism is a procedural account of justice. Instead of defending a specified ideal of justice, necessary features of the setting for deliberation on justice are analyzed. Jürgen Habermas, for instance, reconstructs a situation of deliberation in which each participant, who really engages in a rational conversation, already anticipates a situation in which individuals meet as equal and free. The willingness to listen to arguments presumed individuals come to fair compromises over norms for actions whose consequences accrue to each person.[16] Other universalists rely on a contractualist scenario. Following Rawls, fair principles to distribute particularly important goods as neutral means to a basically good life are the outcome of an initial scenario that is purified from specified interests. Principles of fairness result from a contract that persons enter as moral persons, yet without specified interests or knowledge. In that specific form, universalism results from an initial scenario that is purified from particularities that do not count in terms of justice.[17] Another way to universalism is the argumentation for universal needs or universal values. If universalism is spelled out in objective lists, the argument relies on characterizing a range of items as non-disputable.[18]

Particularists, instead, do not deny the possibility of defending a universal category for measuring justice. But they hold the view that the content of social justice must be chosen case by case. Accordingly, a particularist can defend the view that individuals or groups decide what their most urgent needs are.[19]

The distinction between universalists on the one hand and particularists on the other is of particular importance when efforts are made to relate the concept of public goods to the current debate on justice. It relates to the way arguments for or against public goods can be expressed within the framework of theories on social justice. Arguments that demonstrate a link between public goods and democracy have an empirical and a principled side. In discussing the favorable effects of public goods on central claims of democratic societies, I wish to say that public goods have these effects because of their characteristics. It is not a random link that can be spelled out. Instead, the link itself has an empirical dimension. The claim that public goods are "good for" democracy implies that there is evidence to be found in order to prove that some particularly important democratic structures can be enhanced and general aims of democratic societies can be supported effectively.

Yet, this approach to public goods does not necessarily collapse into *particularism*. Indeed, this would pose a particular problem, since most authors in the field of justice are convinced that principles of justice need to be universal principles. If they were limited to a specific set of conditions, they would not count as principles of justice.

In what follows I shall defend both aspects of the argument. The "currency" that this proposal relies on is the concept of capabilities. This concept takes into account the close tie between background conditions for a basically good life and the life plans of individuals. Instead of interpreting living circumstances as mere resources and instead of presupposing neutral means, an idea about a basically good life leads to a specified range of necessary living conditions.[20] Public goods can provide living conditions that are needed to develop a basic set of capabilities. In defending this relation between public goods and claims of social justice, I shall build on Martha Nussbaum's capabilities approach.[21]

As for universalism vs. particularism, I shall argue that an underlying principle can be justified. It states that each person should be in the position to profit to some degree from goods that can meet the conditions of open access and basic availability. It is a universal principle, but not an unconditional one.

A PRINCIPLE OF FAIRNESS

The *principle of fairness* that I shall defend in this section and the following section says: A good should be provided as a public good when it meets three conditions:

1. The item belongs to a group of goods that are particularly necessary for people to develop a basically good life;
2. The structure of that item as a public good (open access condition and basic availability condition) is due to processes of democratization; in turn the item is part of the success story of societal progress; and
3. The provision of that item as a public good does not result in burdens for a society that are particularly hurtful to be carried.

This principle expresses the normative claim that some goods should be provided as public goods. When the characteristics of public goods are taken in, the principle says: Individuals should not be excluded from goods that are critical to a basically good life of each person, that are part of societal progress in terms of democratization, and that can be provided without producing severe burdens. Moreover, these goods should be made available to each person to some degree.

The reasons for that principle are *not* that each person wishes to avert risks that she might confront throughout her life. Public goods do not follow the logic of goods that serve social security. The reason is neither exclusively that each person wants to make sure that she can—to some degree—fulfill her individual life plan. Instead, the reason is that it would not be right to exclude any person from central goods that *can* be provided as public goods. It expresses the view that it would not be right to burden individuals with one of the toughest experiences. It is the experience to be excluded from participation in benefits that are needed to lead a basically good life and that can, in fact, be made available by common efforts.[22]

Whether or not the burdens are low depends on many different factors. In particular, it is related to economic development. This has to be presupposed to make goods like health care, education, and infrastructure available on a broad scale. It might also depend on institutions that are ready to protect public goods and to provide a regulatory framework. Yet, the amount of burdens alone does not give a sufficient rationale for or against public goods. A hypothetical calculus that leads individuals to vote for public goods, even when they cause costs, works under the condition that the availability of public goods is considered a societal achievement. The stories of social justice that have been recalled at the beginning of this chapter need to be part of the identity of citizens. Yet, the most crucial point is the first condition. I shall now embark on this point.

CENTRAL PUBLIC GOODS

Public goods do not only relate to demands of social justice; moreover, I shall now defend the view that some central public goods can be listed. They are central in the sense that they provide background conditions for what Martha C. Nussbaum terms the "central functional capabilities" of human beings. In arguing with the capabilities of Martha Nussbaum, I shall rely on her notion of the good life and go back to the idea that there is a minimum level that each person should have a chance to realize. Yet, I shall depart from her approach in distinguishing this claim from another, more far-reaching claim. It is the claim that political institutions are obliged to provide the necessary background conditions for that kind of individual development. In my view, it suffices to explain the relationship between justice and public goods. This supports the argument that political actors and civil actors are free to accept or to reject investments in public goods.

According to Martha Nussbaum's capabilities approach, each person should be supported with regard to the development of some central human capabilities.[23] This is the claim of social justice that political institutions should be asked to fulfill. At some point, individual developments can reach a level whose achievement is a precondition for being free to choose and realize a good life according to individual plans and wishes. Up to this point, citizens need to be supported. The basic level of central human functionings is related to the concept of human dignity. A basically good life, that is a life in dignity, results from being in a situation to develop a range of innate capabilities to a degree that is basic to choosing a specific life plan. This implies being in a situation to realizing capabilities in a humane way. Human beings differ from other living beings in that they have a distinct range of capacities and in that they fulfill their capacities in a specific way. Furthermore, the conditions for a basically good life can be spelled out beyond national and cultural borders. Yet, Nussbaum does not defend an unmodified universalism. Instead, universalism means that according to the method of a deliberative equilibrium, humans can come to a conclusion as for a list of most basic capabilities.

For illuminating the relation between the capabilities approach and public goods, it is helpful to state two preconditions of Martha Nussbaum's approach to social justice explicitly. The *first premise* is that people cannot develop a good life unless both internal and external preconditions are available to help develop central capabilities. It also has to be said that, following Nussbaum, an acknowledgment of this kind of dependency of people on living circumstances and on the development of basic dispositions is an assumption that does not undermine but, rather, supports the idea of individual freedom in choosing and developing a good life. Nor does it take away the responsibility of each person with regard to developing an autonomously led life. Instead, it draws attention to dependencies individuals have to cope with and reveals presuppositions of freedom. The *second premise* refers to the idea of development itself. People are regarded as having the potential for developing capacities to lead a good life. Skills that are necessary to realize a basically good life do not spring spontaneously from experiences people make, but have to be trained and experienced. Nevertheless, a good life does not culminate in a shared ideal. It rather is the outcome of individual choices and an individual life plan. Capabilities do not substitute liberties; instead, they are preconditions of liberty.

The list of basic central capabilities that Nussbaum provides includes a specification of central human functional capabilities that refer to the items: life (with which Nussbaum alludes to a normal life span), bodily health, bodily integrity, the senses, imagination, thought, emotions, practical reason, affiliation, other species, play, and control over one's environment.[24] Regarding each sphere of life, a basically good development and realization that suffices for choosing and realizing a fully good life can be identified. According to Nussbaum, "combined capabilities" that have been listed result from internal capabilities, combined with "suitable external conditions for the exercise of the function."[25] "Internal capabilities" are defined as "developed states of the person herself that are, so far as the person herself is concerned, sufficient conditions for the exercise of the requisite functions."[26]

One important trait of the capabilities list is that the combination of internal and external factors is not completely random. Due to this, favorable external conditions can be spelled out when a list of basic functional capabilities is available. The category of public goods comes into the picture when the link between specified individual benefits and background institutions is taken seriously. The benefits that public goods regimes offer are not random, but rather depend on the type of good that is made available as a public good. In addition, access barriers are removed to a degree that allows individuals to partake in the benefits on a basic level.

The list of public goods that relate to basic functional capabilities includes domestic security for the protection of life and integrity of the body; basic infrastructure devices to guarantee freedom of movement; institutions that provide health care; institutions of education; cultural goods for the development of imagination and thought[27] and as a means to educate the practical and theoretical intelligence; environmental goods for guaranteeing the very possibility of relation to animals, plants and the world of nature; institutions for recreation and culture to cultivate play and aesthetic experiences. This list is not as comprehensive as Martha Nussbaums's capabilities list. This results from the fact that it is restricted to material external living conditions that support the development of capabilities, while Nussbaum's list represents capabilities that to some degree have to be protected by institutions that do not offer benefits, but guarantee rights and social order.

The outcome is that although different societies and different local communities will spell out preconditions in different ways, it is possible to correlate specific favorable conditions to specifically human functional capabilities. In this regard, the capabilities approach helps to identify those goods that can be called "central goods" in terms of social justice.

THE DISTRIBUTIVE PARADIGM RECONSIDERED

Introducing public goods to the debate on social justice enriches the ongoing debate. Yet, it also shifts the focus slightly. More important than patterns of distribution are conditions of equal access to a specific range of goods. Instead of focusing on overall useful means for realizing an individual life plan, goods that provide a specified range of basically good living conditions are at stake.

In this section on social justice I wish to demonstrate how the public goods approach to social justice relates to distributive accounts of social justice. I shall argue that the public goods approach does not only accommodate some of the most important claims of distributive accounts. It also helps overcome a systematic limitation that distributive accounts are confronted with.

If goods are defined as public goods, they will be available to all sorts of people, independent of their status or income. One effect of public goods regimes is portrayed quickly. Even if public schools are intended to be open to all, their provision will be most fruitful for those in need. Providing public goods has the effect of being especially favorable to those who could not afford a private provision of them. Furthermore, a positive side effect of including people in need by providing public goods is that it is not necessary to appeal to solidarity. The rationale provided by a public goods approach highlights the benefits for all members of society. People who are in the fortunate position to provide exclusive and private education, health care, or security for themselves are still free to do that. This shift of the focus, however, does not amount to a comprehensive account regarding concerns in terms of social justice. It does not render programs to fight desperate situations superfluous. Public goods can help prevent situations of desperate need, but they do not suffice for persons who have already entered a situation of poverty.

A second perspective on public goods which draws both on the differences and the close link between the claim for public goods and claims for just distribution emphasizes that some public goods are likely to provide preconditions for equal opportunity to acquire more exclusive goods.[28] Although one must accept that the distribution and acquisition of private goods has its own logic, this logic should not hold for those goods that figure as preconditions for access to all kinds of goods. Without infrastructure as a public good, without free access to information and basic education, the access both to economic goods and to socially valued goods is not manageable. Even though these effects do not accrue to all types of goods, the possibility of specifying a list of public goods that serves social justice in terms of capability development, also allows the mention of these effects. Some public goods provide access conditions to exclusive goods. This—as an effect—will also push market distributions in the direction of more equality.

The rationale for demanding public goods is different from the rationale for fairness in distribution. What has been shown so far is that a public goods approach nevertheless shares concerns with Rawlsian and post-Rawlsian theories of justice. The first point alludes to the claim that those being worse off should be considered explicitly and included in distributional affairs. They should also be privileged by focusing on diminishing their burdens. The second point expresses the view that all participants of a political community should be provided equally with opportunities to acquire goods of high values.

After having discussed similarities, I shall now discuss a major difference between a public goods approach and distributive approaches on justice. One crucial question for distributive accounts is where to draw the critical line between already existing patterns of distribution that are acceptable and those that have to be corrected. For this purpose, demanding equality is not sufficient. What we wish to see is not equality in total terms; no one demands that resources, chances, or outcomes really converge. What we rather wish to see is a criterion for drawing the line between which kind and amount of redistribution can duly be expected to find approval by all members of society. If comparisons in terms of urgency of needs or in terms of real achievements shall be avoided,[29] a criterion that remains is the distinction between what lies within and without the boundaries of *personal responsibility*.[30] The problem that immediately surfaces is not that this criterion is far-fetched. One might share the intuition that if people achieve something with all their efforts it really is earned, and that it is unfair if people fail despite their best efforts. The core problem rather is to spell out what this criterion really means. At this point, distributive accounts come to a systematic limit. There simply is no perspective from which to judge neutrally whether or not people have caused the trouble they are in, we do not possess God's eye.

Ronald Dworkin presents a solution for this conflict within his resource-oriented approach to justice that is exemplary for the dilemma that results from rendering the responsibility threshold more precise without being in a situation to find firm grounds for doing so.[31] Dworkin tries to figure out what equal respect and equal concern that should be guaranteed to all citizens in the design of political institutions actually means. After having stated that the government should treat all those in its charge as equals and after having acknowledged that a system of rights has to be supplemented by a system of distribution of resources, he still has to draw the line between the content of what citizens should receive as equals and what lies beyond that line. Even though nobody can correct distributions to the point of eliminating all random factors, it is possible to distinguish between what Dworkin calls "option luck" and "brute luck." The distinction must be seen against the background of Dworkin's defense of equality of resources and the idea of an auction that has already led to a redistribution of assets according to individual tastes.[32] It leads to a distribution that is satisfactory for each person in that she will no longer envy the bundle of goods of any other person. Here is the distinction of option luck and brute luck:

> Option luck is a matter of how deliberate and calculated gambles turn out—whether someone gains or losses through accepting an isolated

> risk he or she should have anticipated and might have declined. Brute luck is a matter of how risks fall out that are not in that sense deliberate gambles. If I buy a stock on the exchange that rises, then my option luck is good. If I am hit by a falling meteorite whose course could not have been predicted, then my bad luck is brute (even though I could have moved just before it struck if I had had any reason to know where it would strike).[33]

The distinction and what it is intended to say are clear. Whereas it may well lie within my responsibility to take a risk that is embedded in situations of option luck, nobody can be held responsible for situations of brute bad luck. The question that now arises is how this distinction bears on the further distinction between what is part of *social* responsibility and what lies beyond it. In other words: What orientation does the distinction of option luck and brute luck provide regarding corrective interventions of political institutions in favor of social justice?

This example shows that although the basic distinction between acceptable outcomes that rely on the decisions of responsible actors and non-acceptable outcomes that do not is plausible, it is difficult to translate the initial intuition into a sensible scheme of distribution and corrections of a current situation.[34] Starting with the market system itself is not a systematically reliable possibility either. There is no "invisible hand" generating good, or at least acceptable, outcomes for all.[35] Many authors have pointed to this flaw inherent in market systems.[36] Incentives for best performances and rewards for excellent ideas and particular skills are basics of the system, and so are inequalities. A more convincing focus, not only to overcome these notorious problems, but also to provide people with the motivation to actually contribute to bearing the burdens of provision, is the focus on public goods.

PUBLIC GOODS AS SOCIAL EQUALIZERS

In this chapter I have argued that it is not fair to withhold a basic provision of security, cultural goods, environmental goods, education, health care, and infrastructure from any person. The normative claim regarding these goods, as expressed in this chapter, is that—for reasons of fairness—each person should have an equal chance to access these goods on a basic level. The underlying rationale is not the idea of a contract, nor is it a calculation of benefits and losses. I have argued that it results from an understanding of social justice that interprets equal access to basic goods as a regulative idea.

I shall conclude with an illustration that opens the discussion toward a direction that has not been followed in this chapter. Mr. Penalosa, the former Mayor of Bogota, who now gives advice to city planners, began to establish public goods in the poorest neighborhoods of Bogota. He built public libraries, installed sidewalks so that people could go for a walk and public parks for spending leisure time. Mr. Penalosa understands public goods not only as necessary means to realize justice, but as an essential ingredient in what he calls a "politics of happiness." He summarizes his experiences as follows: "Parks have a very powerful role to play as equalizers of society. We almost always meet under conditions of social hierarchy. At work, some people are bosses, and others are employees; at restaurants, some people are serving and others are being served. Parks are the gathering place for community. They create a sense of belonging. Everybody is welcome regardless of age, background, income, or disabilities. This creates a different type of society."[37]

NOTES

1. The importance of distributional ideas resulting from assumptions about "cooperative societies" is reiterated in John Rawls, *Political Liberalism* (New York: Columbia University Press, 1996). After having explained that cooperation "is different from merely socially coordinated activity," Rawls continues: "A conception of political justice characterizes the fair terms of cooperation. Since the primary subject of justice is the basic structure of society, these fair terms are expressed by principles that specify basic rights and duties within its main institutions and regulate the arrangements of background justice over time, so that the benefits produced by everyone's efforts are fairly distributed and shared from one generation to the next. The idea of social cooperation requires an idea of each participant's rational advantage, or good." Rawls, *Political Liberalism*, 16. The list of "primary social goods" that includes "rights and liberties, opportunities and powers, income and wealth" and "self-esteem" is presented

in John Rawls, *A Theory of Justice* (Cambridge, MA: Harvard University Press, 1971), 92; and the slightly modified and more specified list of primary social goods in Rawls, *Political Liberalism*, 181.

2. Rawls, *A Theory of Justice*, 332. For a comparable statement *see* Rawls, *Political Liberalism*, 214–215.

3. For a list of these central human functional capabilities *see* Martha C. Nussbaum, *Women and Human Development: The Capabilities Approach* (Cambridge, UK: Cambridge University Press, 2000), 78–80.

4. I call it a "story," because other people from other cultural and historical backgrounds would probably tell a different story; my story is based on developments in Western societies.

5. For a historical account on the roots of the German welfare state and its development until today *see* Gabriele Metzler, *Der deutsche Sozialstaat: Vom Bismarckschen Erfolgsmodell zum Pflegefall* (Stuttgart and München: Deutsche Verlags-Anstalt, 2003). The evolvement of the social security system is discussed in Metzler, *Der deutsche Sozialstaat*, 16–37. Metzler points out that the three basic laws assuring assistance of the state in the case of illness (Krankenversicherungsgesetz, 1883), accidents (Unfallversicherungsgesetz, 1884) and invalidity and old age (Invaliditäts-und Altersversicherungsgesetz, 1889) are three pillars of the welfare state. This is the basis that persists in the German welfare state until today. Major supplements have been the unemployment insurance system (Arbeitslosenversicherung, 1927) and the care system for handicapped and elderly people (Pflegeversicherung, 1995).

6. *See* Thomas Nipperdey, *Wie das Bürgertum die Moderne fand* (Berlin: Siedler, 1988).

7. Nipperdey, *Bürgertum*, 22.

8. For this example *see* James T. Patterson, *Grand Expectations: The United States, 1945–1974* (New York and Oxford: Oxford University Press, 1996), 400–405.

9. For an analysis of the *normative* ideas and concepts related to welfare goods *see also* Robert E. Goodin, *Reasons for Welfare: The Political Theory of the Welfare State* (Princeton, NJ: Princeton University Press, 1988).

10. For Rawls's list of primary goods *see* Rawls, *A Theory of Justice*, 90–94.

11. *See* Michael Walzer, *Spheres of Justice: A Defense of Pluralism and Equality* (New York: Basic Books, 1983).

12. In choosing the term "currency," I allude to a contribution of Cohen who distinguishes approaches to social justice along the chosen point of comparison. *See* Gerald A. Cohen, "On the Currency of Egalitarian Justice," *Ethics* 99 (1989): 906–944.

13. According to a broad understanding of "resources," both Dworkin and Rawls count as resourcists. Dworkin's approach was first presented in: Ronald Dworkin, "What Is Equality? Part II: Equality of Resources," *Philosophy and Public Affairs* 10 (1981): 283–345. For Rawls's list of primary goods *see* John Rawls, *A Theory of Justice*, 90–94. A more detailed discussion is given in Rawls, *Political Liberalism*, 178–190.

14. For a defense of the possibility to calculate preferences, which is the precondition for distributive subjectivism, *see* Richard J. Arneson, "Equality and Equal Opportunity for Welfare," *Philosophical Studies* 56 (1989): 77–93. An early version of distributive subjectivism was presented by Thomas M. Scanlon who argued that urgent preferences can be filtered and interpersonal comparisons be made transparent. Thomas M. Scanlon, "Preference and Urgency," *Journal of Philosophy* 72 (1975): 655–669. More recently, Scanlon came closer to a more objective approach in that he argued that some goods are desirable in themselves. Individuals should not withhold goods that are desirable from each other. Thomas M. Scanlon, *What We Owe to Each Other* (Cambridge, MA, and London, UK: Belknap Press of Harvard University Press, 1998).

15. For a recent defense of the capabilities approach and an outline of its consequences in political philosophy and in animal ethics *see* Martha C. Nussbaum, *Frontiers of Justice: Disability, Nationality, Species Membership* (Cambridge, MA: Harvard University Press, 2006).

16. For a restatement of his discourse theory, see Jürgen Habermas, "A Genealogical Analysis of the Cognitive Content of Morality," in *The Inclusion of the Other: Studies in Political Philosophy*, ed. C. Cronin and P. De Greiff (Cambridge, MA: MIT Press, 1998), 3–46.

17. A detailed discussion of Rawls's concept of equality is given in Norman Daniels, "Democratic Equality: Rawls's Complex Egalitarianism," in *The Cambridge Companion to Rawls*, ed. Samuel Freeman (Cambridge, UK, et al.: Cambridge University Press, 2003), 241–276.

18. A defense of universal values that underly a list of capabilities is presented in Nussbaum, *Women and Human Development*, 34–58 and 78–80.

19. Amartya Sen defends particularism regarding the content of justice despite a universal category of justice. Amartya Sen, *Inequality Reexamined* (Oxford: Clarendon Press, and Cambridge, MA: Harvard University Press, 1992), 131–134.

20. Because of the central role of capabilities as achievements, Nussbaum defines the capabilities approach as "an outcome-oriented approach." *See* Nussbaum, *Frontiers of Justice*, 281.

21. Nussbaum discusses the relation of her account to Sen's approach to central capabilities in "Capabilities as Fundamental Entitlements: Sen and

Social Justice," *Feminist Economics* 9, no. 2–3 (2003): 33–59. In this article, Nussbaum criticizes an ambiguity in Sen's writings that results from endorsing some capabilities as "absolutely central and nonnegotiable" while on the other hand, "Sen has conspicuously refused to endorse any account of the central capabilities." Nussbaum, *Capabilities as Fundamental Entitlements,* 43–44. According to Nussbaum, Sen fails to specify capabilities sufficiently. Nussbaum, *Capabilities as Fundamental Entitlements*, 46.

22. In my view, that principle could also be defended within a procedural setting. But that would presuppose some motivational aspects for which I do not have evidence at hand. It could rely on the idea that individuals, whenever possible, try to avoid that experience of exclusion. In contrast, individuals are ready to pay a price not only for public goods, but for a situation in which no one will be excluded from goods that each person could profit from. For sure, individuals are not ready to pay any price for non-exclusion. But they are ready to pay a price when it guarantees a list of public goods. The underlying rationale for individuals to choose public goods is an aversion to non-necessary exclusion.

23. For a discussion of the basic capabilities *see* Nussbaum, *Women and Human Development*. For a discussion of the underlying concept of "capabilities" *see also* Martha C. Nussbaum, "Nature, Function and Capability: Aristotle on Political Distribution," *Oxford Studies in Ancient Philosophy*, suppl. vol. 1 (1988): 145–184; "Aristotelian Social Democracy," *Liberalism and the Good*, ed. R. B. Douglas (New York: Routledge, 1990), 203–252; "Human Functioning and Social Justice: In Defence of Aristotelian Essentialism," *Political Theory* 20 (1992): 202–246. Nussbaum also argues that making laws for the provision of a good also implies that participating in this good can be mandatory. For this problem and examples of tragic conflicts in this respect see Martha Nussbaum, "The Costs of Tragedy: Some Moral Limits of Cost-Benefit Analysis," *Journal of Legal Studies* 29, no. 2 (2000): 1005–1036.

24. For the complete list *see* Nussbaum, *Women and Human Development*, 78–89.

25. Nussbaum, *Women and Human Development*, 85.

26. Nussbaum, *Women and Human Development*, 84.

27. This claim is outlined in detail in Martha C. Nussbaum, *Cultivating Humanity: A Classical Defense of Reform in Liberal Education* (Cambridge, MA: Harvard University Press., 1997).

28. Cass R. Sunstein argues in his contribution on the New Deal for the constitutional relevance of social and economic rights. He also makes a similar point and shows that the provision of education is a precondition for the real opportunity to fully participate in society, a chance that is secured by the guarantee of civil rights. For this argument see Cass R. Sunstein, *The Second Bill*

of Rights: FDR's Unfinished Revolution and Why We Need It More Than Ever (New York: Basic Books, 2004), 184–192. Sunstein also reflects the relationship between negative and positive rights that bears on the problem of how socio-economic rights are related to political and civic rights. Sunstein, *The Second Bill of Rights*, 197–202.

29. Resourcists claim that both should be avoided because they intrude into the realm of private life plans and achievements.

30. One example for the crucial role of this idea is implicit in the defense of the "basic opportunity principle" by Gutman and Thompson—a principle that "would secure citizens an *adequate* level of basic opportunity goods. . . . What policies this principle requires must be left partly to democratic deliberation, but the range of acceptable policies is not unlimited. . . . More positively, basic opportunities should be distributed by standards that fulfill the fundamental purpose of the opportunity principle." Amy Gutmann and Dennis Thompson, *Democracy and Disagreement* (Cambridge, MA and London, UK: Harvard University Press, 1996), 273–274. The central argument for the "basic opportunity principle" is the following: "The essential point is that citizens should not be denied basic opportunities on the basis of factors for which they are not responsible." Gutman and Thompson, *Democracy and Disagreement*, 274.

31. A systematic outline of the theory is given in: Ronald Dworkin, *Sovereign Virtue: The Theory and Practice of Equality* (Cambridge, MA, and London, UK: Harvard University Press, 2000).

32. For this concept *see* Ronald Dworkin, "What Is Equality? Part II: Equality of Resources," *Philosophy and Public Affairs* 10 (1981): 283–290. It is important to acknowledge that Dworkin defends the market mechanism as critical for reaching an optimal auction outcome and regards the "contingent facts of raw material and the distribute of tastes" as not being "grounds on which someone might challenge a distribution as unequal." Dworkin, *Equality II*, 289.

33. *See* Dworkin, *Sovereign Virtue*, 73.

34. To be fair with Dworkin's account, it must be added that he introduces a second differentiation that shall help overcome this difficulty. For being in a position to give an answer, a further distinction has to be taken into account: the distinction between ambition-sensitivity and endowment-sensitivity. "On the one hand we must, on pain of violating equality, allow the distribution of resources at any particular moment to be (as we might say) ambition-sensitive. It must reflect the cost of benefit to others of the choices people make so that, for example, those who choose to invest rather than consume, or to consume less expensively rather than more, or to work in more rather than less profitable ways, must be permitted to retain the gains that flow from the decisions in an equal auction followed by free trade. But on the other hand, we must not

allow the distribution of resources at any moment to be endowment-sensitive, that is, to be affected by differences in ability of the sort that produce income differences in a laissez-faire economy among people with the same ambitions." Dworkin, *Souvereign Virtue*, 310. This distinction, however, also opens up the field of a whole range of new questions. Outcomes in the real world of acquisition are not only dependent on ambition, but equally on talents and preferences that in their turn are the outcome of mixed processes of individual preference building and choices and random environmental influences. These soft factors play an important role, but how are they linked to responsibility? Much more difficult questions could also be posed, questions regarding the boundaries of what "endowment" means. Where is the boundary between accepting something as an "endowment" or changing it, even before a person is born?

35. For the metaphor of the "invisible hand" that symbolizes the unintended side effect of market transactions by pursuing the individual interest, the interest of the society is promoted. *See* Adam Smith, *An Inquiry into the Nature and Causes of the Wealth of Nations*, ed. Edwin Cannan (Chicago: University of Chicago Press, 1976), 477–478.

36. For a technical explanation why the achievement of Pareto efficiency is not necessarily correlated with a social optimum *see* Amartya Sen, "Markets and Freedoms," in *Rationality and Freedom* (Cambridge, MA, and London, UK: Belknap Press of Harvard University Press, 2002), 504–505. The consequence is apparent: "To use the competitive market equilibrium to achieve any social optimum, we have to get the initial distribution of resources right, and depending on how equity-conscious our social objectives are, this could require a total reallocation of ownership patterns from whatever pattern we may have inherited historically." Sen, *Markets and Freedoms*, 505.

37. Enrique Penalosa, "The Politics of Happiness: The Trust for Public Land." A conversation led by Susan Ives, *Land & People* (Fall 2002): 2.

6

POLITICAL SELF-DETERMINATION

In a special issue on democratic development in China, Bruce B. De Mesquita and George W. Downs discuss in which way authoritarian regimes succeed in interrupting processes of democratization.[1] Anti-democratic regimes have an interest to undermine coordination among a democratic-minded opposition.[2] Economic growth is one factor which effectively spurs the chances on strategic coordination: It leads to urbanization and improvements in technology and infrastructure, which in turn facilitates coordination. Yet, even though side effects in terms of democratization are not desired, it would be fatal to jeopardize economic development. Instead, the best way to interrupt democratization appears to consist in "carefully rationing a particular subset of public goods—goods that are crucial to political coordination but less important for economic cooperation."[3]

According to De Mesquita and Downs, examples of that strategy to interrupt processes of democratization abound. China has restricted Internet-related activities; in Russia, the government has placed all national TV networks under strict government control; in Venezuela, President Hugo Chavez controls broadcasting licenses of the media. The dominant pattern to oppress an opposition includes restrictions in public transportation, health care, primary education, and even in national defense.[4] This pattern was also frequently established in Asia and Africa until the 1980s, and in poorer countries it is still employed. The major reason why some public goods are spared is the aversive effect on economic development.

These examples demonstrate an intricate link between public goods and processes of democratic development. Theories on public goods, however, draw a different picture. Instead of discussing public goods regarding their function in democracy, participatory and legitimatory gaps have been of central concern.[5] In this chapter, my central aim is to draw attention to another line of thought. Although it is necessary to think about the improvement of political participation in shaping public goods regimes, public goods also function as an important ingredient in processes of political self-determination. In particular, there is a close relation between a self-confident civil society and self-determination in establishing and shaping public goods.

Before getting started, something has to be said about the concept of political self-determination. In theories on democracies, political self-determination is a central issue.[6] One way of clarifying this concept starts with discussing the general meaning of "democracy."[7] On a general level, democracy can be identified as a form of government which attempts to reconcile two different claims. *First*, democracy is a form of government that responds to collective interests. In that respect, political self-determination can be identified with the idea that political decisions express the will of the people. Thus, political self-determination is used synonymously to popular sovereignty and its institutional representation in terms of free elections and a representative political system. *Secondly*, democracy relates to a set of political values. In particular, the equality of all citizens in basic respects and a basic system of freedoms will be guaranteed.

This interpretation of democracy corresponds to two meanings of self-determination. As for the *first* meaning of democracy, political self-determination will be realized in terms of political representation. Yet the link between political representation and public goods has primarily been negative. Public goods regimes have been considered particularly problematic because they affect each citizen's life. Mechanisms such as the unanimity rule and political strategies for direct democracy have been invented to improve political participation in public goods regimes. I shall discuss these strategies in *section one* and *two* of this chapter. In *section three* I shall turn to the link between public goods and political self-determination that corresponds to the second sense of "democracy." Self-determination then says that a citizenry is free to build its own public goods and even to express its identity through public goods regimes. This perspective has several implications. I shall discuss the view that a selection of public goods helps guarantee the worth of more basic rights. In *section four* I shall present an alternative account. It claims that public goods support the political self-determination of the citizenship in that they provide a focus for the common concerns of civil society. This leads to an idea of democracy that will be spelled out in *section five*. It deserves the name "committed democracy."

THE UNANIMITY RULE RECONSIDERED

It is easy to see that each citizen will be—more or less directly—affected by public goods policies. These effects result from the necessity to finance public goods; and they result from the need to introduce regulatory frameworks. Even though it is open to discussion how far-reaching these techniques are and whether or not they can be avoided, there is no question that public goods need some of these institutional background arrangements.

In theories on democratic performances, the deep impact of policies that come with the establishment of public goods has been reflected. In its strictest form, agreement on public goods translates as a call for unanimous decisions. A unanimity rule for that kind of decision was already proposed in 1896 by Knut Wicksell.[8] Wicksell was primarily interested in fiscal policy. Yet, he acknowledged the need for a transparent scheme which justified taxes. Expenditure of public finance should be scrutinized in detail and the outcomes of that examination should be made public. For each expenditure project of the state, different allocation proposals should be elaborated. Only in case of a unanimous approval of a post-constitutional assembly, a specific policy could be realized. A democratically chosen parliament is best in fulfilling this objective. In social choice theory, a unanimity proposal has been reconsidered by Gordon Tullock and James Buchanan. They also believe that unanimous statements can be elaborated. Therefore, calculations regarding the costs and losses that result from different schemes should be elaborated.[9]

The more general idea that crystallizes in the proposal of a unanimity rule is that if citizens cannot flee the consequences of policies—and they actually cannot if public goods are subsidized by means of public finance and accompanied by regulatory frameworks—the need for a consensual agreement on them is mandatory. Even though the initial idea is understandable, the idea of a post-constitutional contract which leads to unanimous decisions must be criticized. One of the major problems is that unanimity is an unrealistic expectation.[10] The best one can hope for in existing democracies is a reasonable compromise. In answer to this problem, proposals have been made to avoid unrealistic expectations regarding public goods policies.[11] Therefore, social choice theorists and political philosophers have chosen a different path to work on what has been called a "participatory gap."

One way to do so consists in outlining uncontroversial criteria that help settle disputes over public goods.[12] The contractual position of Buchanan implies the recommendation to turn to neutral standards and calculate the costs of several options. This option is echoed by authors who favor economic calculation as a guide to political decisions on public goods. The proposal implies that costs which result from public goods regimes should be calculated and compared with alternative policies. Costs for public goods, for instance, imply costs of regulation. A comparison of costs for public goods and costs for private goods can lead to the insight that private goods are the cheaper solution.

A more sophisticated approach turns to social costs. A calculus shall demonstrate how the problems resulting from unrealistic expectations regarding unanimity might be settled. When a good is organized as a collective good, two different sets of costs must be expected: the "pain of excluding non-owners" on the one, and the "difficulty of coordination between co-owners" on the other hand. To establish a good as a public good is recommended if the costs for exclusion of non-owners trump the costs for coordination between co-owners.[13] If all individuals have an interest in an environmental good, for instance, but cannot come to an end in negotiating over that good, it might be the best solution for all to establish the good as a public good and interrupt negotiation.

One problem with this approach is that public goods are defined as goods that are owned by groups of people. In that respect, the definition applied in the example deviates from our definition of a public good. In addition, it has to be asked: Does that calculation really give a clue to what citizens agree upon when it comes to best policies regarding waterways, rivers, highways, and broadcasting?[14] And how shall the costs of exclusion be calculated if individuals have not yet made the experience of being excluded? To substitute some kind of allegedly neutral method of calculus for democratic decision-making procedures is not a convincing proposal. The conclusion of this section is that neither unanimity nor neutral calculation can convincingly resolve the problem of legitimatory gaps.

HEALING PARTICIPATORY DEFICITS

Instead of demanding unanimity, authors have discussed methods to improve the conditions for political self-determination regarding public goods regimes. Along these lines, instruments of direct democracy have been regarded as a remedy for participatory deficits. On the first glance, this appears to be a reasonable alternative. Bruce Ackermann's and James S. Fishkin's plea for a nation-wide "deliberation day" has initiated a broad debate on means for improving devices of participation in political processes.[15] A "deliberation day" might inform citizens about differences in political agendas, it might stimulate debates on political issues and it might strengthen participation in responsibility of political goals. As a result of Deliberative Polling—a device that has already been tested[16]—an example that underscores the reliability of this expectation can be given. It demonstrates changes that occurred after deliberation polls over future energy politics. Consumers of Texas petrol were asked about their ideas on power for the future. Averaged over all eight deliberation polls that were employed, the percentage of participants who were willing to pay more for renewable energy rose from 52 to 84 percent; respondents were also willing to pay more to support conservation programs and subsidies for low-income customers.[17]

Although one has to be cautious about these outcomes—a poll can only portray what people say they are willing to contribute and does not show what they actually will contribute—it is apparent that more direct participation in public goods policies will have an effect on the legitimacy of public goods policies. Citizens are much more directly involved in decision-making procedures than through election alone. Ackerman and Fishkin note "that discussion leads respondents to take some responsibility for the solution of public problems. They look beyond the most narrow and immediate constructions of their self-interest to support the provision of public goods."[18]

Defenders of direct democracy demand that decisions on health care, education, and infrastructure should be carried out by those individuals who are affected by them. As a consequence, self-government regarding essential common goods is considered the best solution. The biggest problem with these proposals is that direct democracy is difficult to attain in nations that comprise millions of citizens. In our understanding, it is a central characteristic of public goods that individuals can freely and voluntarily choose whether to access them or not. As an effect, public goods are different from club goods. One of the challenges of demanding devices of direct democracy is the scale on which this would have to happen.

This challenge has already been acknowledged. As a consequence, defenders of democratic public goods regimes try to break policies down to a group level. These groups can be identified as interest groups that constitute themselves on a local level.[19] This solution, however, is not appropriate in another respect: public goods lose one of their most important features when delegated to interest groups. Public goods are now reserved to communities that govern themselves; they are no longer public goods. Another problem is that proposals for communal self-governance fall short of acknowledging the complexity of policymaking procedures and the need for regulation which reaches beyond the local level. Even if local communities cared for a good environment, health care, or schools—they would still depend on legislation on the state level. Participatory gaps have to be closed on each level of public goods provision. When the global dimension of current public goods is taken seriously, this leads to demanding agencies that care for political participation on each level of political organization.

In the reminder of this chapter, I shall embark on a different approach to public goods and democracy. In my view, one of the major shortfalls of the discussion is the focus on participatory and legitimatory gaps. Instead, the more general question has to be asked: *What impact do public goods policies have on democracies?* Obviously, there is a complex link between democracy and public goods. That link cannot be reduced to claims for legitimacy and participation. Rather, the provision of public goods is also related to what citizens are justified to expect from democratic states. In addition, it appears as if not only the freedom to participate in decisions over public goods, but also the freedom to provide for public goods is an essential ingredient in democratic freedoms.

For elaborating on these ideas, I shall first give a brief discussion of the complex link between claims for public goods and basic rights. I cannot unfold that debate within the frame of this chapter; instead, my more modest aim is to remind us of a debate that already demonstrates the commitment of democracies to a specified range of public goods. Secondly, I shall discuss the link between public goods and democratic ideals of freedom and self-determination. This leads to a reassessment of the roles of governments as related to the role of civil society in democracies. I shall argue that in democracies, civil society is free to reinvent itself through public goods.

PUBLIC GOODS AND RIGHTS

As for the relationship between basic rights and public goods, one thing appears to be obvious: Political protection and support of public goods differs from human rights policies. Human rights need to be protected, public goods need to be built and intentionally pursued. Public goods policies focus on schools that have to be built, on infrastructure that has to be sustained, and on public places that have to be redeveloped from time to time. At least regarding the group of civil rights, governments instead guarantee to protect individuals. This implies the guarantee to *refrain from* interfering with activities of individuals. The difference between actively establishing and building a material good and respecting the actions and authorship of individuals is obvious and cannot be questioned.[20]

Yet, a closer look reveals that the differences between both kinds of political regimes are not as big as one might think. This becomes clear in turning to the background of what is needed in protecting basic rights. In *The Cost of Rights: Why Liberty Depends on Taxes*, Stephen Holmes and Cass R. Sunstein argue that the protection of rights actually is a costly and a managerially demanding enterprise.[21] From that perspective, the difference between public goods policies and the protection of rights shrinks. It also no longer coincides with the differences between pursued political goals on the one hand and self-limitation of governments on the other hand. Instead, activities involved in public goods policies and in the protection of basic rights are in some respects similar to each other. Both are costly, both need regulation and both cannot be restricted to rules of non-interference with private activities.

Yet, these similarities should not be overstated. Public goods and their provision depend to a high degree on concrete economic and political circumstances. The protection of basic rights, instead, can be fulfilled even if a country does not belong to the groups of economically developed countries.[22]

So far, differences and similarities between public goods and human rights regimes have been scrutinized on an empirical level. A new perspective opens up when the reassessment of both starts from a normative point of view. On normative grounds, a close tie between public goods and basic human rights can be drawn from debate over the relationship between rights of the first generation and so-called rights of the second generation. The latter, socioeconomic rights can be interpreted as a group of rights that round up the program of basic rights in that they guarantee living circumstances that are necessary for actually profiting from first-generation rights. It can be argued that freedom of movement cannot be guaranteed without also establishing infrastructure and public transport. The freedom of self-expression is not effectively guaranteed, unless a good educational system cares for the literacy and education of individuals, and so forth.[23] In short, a right to a specified range of public goods is a necessary supplement to civic and political rights.[24] In that view, public goods are the material instruments that are necessary to realize the promised freedoms. In that perspective, public goods come close to the so-called second-generation rights.

Yet, things are more complicated than that. Public goods can be used and abused by groups as well as by political institutions and the government. Precisely because public goods serve basic needs of individuals, dependencies can easily be exploited. One of the most important questions regarding public goods and democracy is how democracies can prepare themselves for averting these perils without giving up the commitment to public goods. Instead of listing public goods and entitlements to public goods as an addendum to civic and political rights, the so-called first-generation rights must also be considered as *complementary* to the entitlements to public goods. Without the protection of civic and political rights, citizens cannot be protected from abuse of public goods by political bodies and voluntary associations.

In reassessing the link between public goods and basic human rights, I have tried to stress similarities and differences. Both concepts have to be kept apart even though there are connections that tie them together. These brief comments on public goods and rights are no more than cursory. The debate on rights is a complex debate, and it would take more analysis to give a precise account of which goods actually are related to which group of basic entitlements. In the remainder of this chapter, I shall try to go beyond this already well-established perspective and discuss the democratic ideal of self-determination from a different angle.

SELF-DETERMINATION RECONSIDERED

Democracy means that people have the chance to live as they wish. This premise was already established by Aristotle, albeit in a critical voice, who defined it as one of the two pillars of democracy.[25] The commitment to civic freedoms is critical to democracy. Yet, it can be interpreted in two completely different ways. In political liberalism, freedom primarily means the freedom to live as each individual chooses to live. Philosophers as diverse as Locke, Mill, and Bentham were all committed to this ideal.[26] In contrast to the tradition of political liberalism, civic republicanism as portrayed in the history of political philosophy stresses political freedom as the freedom of self-determination. In order to call a country democratic, citizens must have the chance to get actively involved in its government. Freedom means self-determination through political participation. Moreover, civic virtues contribute to shaping the political community.[27]

This alternative can be portrayed as an answer to two different problems. Political liberalism is concerned with the problem of how political power can be contained so that governments do not infringe unduly on the citizens' liberties. Civic republicanism, instead, primarily gives answers to the question of how aspirations of the citizenry to be an active part within a state and to realize an ideal of "good citizenship" can be fulfilled.[28] Both aspects have become an integral part of current approaches on democracy. They also represent two different lines of thought regarding the concept of self-determination. In political liberalism, self-determination translates into the mechanisms of a representative political institution that respects the freedom of citizens; in civic republicanism, self-determination of the citizenry is realized when citizens have a direct vote regarding common projects. Following the second line of thought, self-determination is realized in forms of collective management of public goods.

Yet, both theoretical approaches on democracy and the ideal of self-determination rely on simplification. They both abstract from the thick layer of private and political institutions "in between" the citizenry and the state. Whether or not one subscribes to theories of modernity, one thing cannot be denied: Citizens participate in many different ways in complex societal systems that differ from living in a family and bonds of kinship and from political society and political institutions. Citizens unfold their activities within the realm of civil society.

The claim that I wish to render plausible in the remainder of this section is the idea that within this realm public goods play an important role. First, they provide focal points for debate on issues of common concern; secondly, they are a medium in which the citizenry realizes self-determination in a specified way: In competing over the provision of public goods and in building public goods, a citizenry defines its identity. Goods that fulfill these functions particularly well shall be called *identification goods*.

The *first part* of the thesis claims that public goods support civil society in the articulation of common concerns. Public goods differ from private goods in that they do not have access barriers with selective effects. Instead, each person can to some degree profit from a public good. Normally, interests in these goods are not a harmonious whole; instead, different interest groups will have ideas about a common good that conflict with each other. A river serves as a good example: Some people like to go fishing on the weekend; industry wishes to take the water for processes of industrial production; other people might like to see it as a protected natural area in which a rich flora flourishes, and so forth. The peculiarity that comes with the river as a public good is that dividing it into several parts that allow different ways of profiting from it does not work. Instead, some kind of compromise must be developed regarding differing interests. This example teaches an interesting lesson.

Different from other conflicts, conflicts over public goods do not start from scratch. First of all, they are about specified goods whose shape or existence is at stake. This is important for giving the conflict a distinct shape and a particular content. Secondly, people engage in the conflict not as disinterested observers, but as potential beneficiaries. Dissent over public goods is not a children's game, it provokes debate. But it also needs to come to an end at some point. In contrast to conflicts that do not need to be settled, public goods regimes force a compromise at some point. When it is taken into account, that "societies need dissent," public goods serve an important aim.[29] This thesis does not claim that public goods regimes themselves provide a civilized realm for debate. This is something that has to be provided as an institutional frame within which conflicts can be played out. But it claims that public goods will provide focal points of public debate.

The *second part* of this thesis says something about a mechanism that can best be described as the possibility of a virtuous circle within civil society. Again, an example may introduce the central idea. In discussing the culture of public parks in American cities, Janet Jacobs articulates an interesting finding. She describes a former situation in which parks were in a poor state. They became meeting places for the drug and crime scene. She contrasts this situation with one in which a park is a flourishing place of mixed communities. And she comes to an interesting conclusion. The key for explaining the difference is the level of identification with this park that citizens developed. When citizens identify with a park and consider it their mutual "property," they also care for it and engage in cultivating that area. In the best case, something like what Jacobs calls a *virtuous circle* can be realized: The public park becomes a nice place when citizens like it. In turn, this motivates citizens to contribute to taking care of that place.[30] Another important factor is the distribution of space within a park. Each group needs a particular place to identify with. In benefitting from these "niches," citizens learn to accept each other's "niches." This example teaches a lesson about public goods. They can serve as identification goods when citizens consider them "their" goods.

COMMITTED DEMOCRACY

One dilemma democracies have to resolve is that practices in favor of some ideas on the common good pull into one direction, whereas the respect for individual freedom pushes into the other direction. In my view, public goods can help resolve that tension. *First* of all, public goods do not represent a version of the common weal that presupposes shared values. Public goods are not moral goods.[31] Instead, they are defined by specific functions they can fulfill in terms of underpinning the public, enhancing conditions of social justice, and serving as identification goods. In order to fulfill these functions, it is neither necessary for each person to attach the same value to that good, nor do public goods need to be thought of as neutral zones. Instead, the existence of public goods contributes to a situation that stimulates compromise; moreover, they can help the citizenry to develop points of identification. *Secondly*, to expect unanimity is demanding too much. If civil society is committed to public goods, unanimity is not even a necessary idea. As long as associations take some responsibility, diversity of public goods can also be expected.

Instead of interpreting concepts of self-determination exclusively as expressing ideas of political participation, I have argued that the concept of self-determination must be understood in a broader sense. It also relates to processes within the realm of civil society. Public goods enter the picture as focal points for the process of self-determination in terms of shaping common sense. The thesis that public goods can serve as identification goods can also be expressed in terms of democracy: Democracy is a situation in which a citizenry is free to reinvent itself through public goods. The process of reinvention does not come to an end at any point. Instead, a continuous effort to shape and reshape public goods is necessary.[32] That process has two dimensions. In participating in public goods and in contributing to them, citizens shape their common goods; they also shape them in publicly debating on them and developing compromises.

The arguments that I have presented in this chapter also amount to a lesson about democracies that theories on human rights has already been learned. Democracy is confronted with the paradoxical demand to a continued restitution of its living conditions. Today, to care for mechanisms that prevent the accumulation of power in one hand and to care for rights that protect citizens from state power does no longer suffice. Instead, citizens should take the chance to build their *identification goods* instead of exclusively relying on support by state institutions.

NOTES

1. Bruce Bruno De Mesquita and George W. Downs, "Development and Democracy," *Foreign Affairs* 84, no. 5 (September/October 2005): 77–86.
2. De Mesquita and Downs, *Development*, 80.
3. De Mesquita and Downs, *Development*, 81.
4. De Mesquita and Downs, *Development*, 82.
5. Recent contributions to public goods react to three kinds of "gaps": a jurisdictional gap, a participation gap, and an incentive gap. All three gaps are explained in the introduction of: Inge Kaul, Isabelle Grunberg, and Marc A. Stern, eds., *Global Public Goods: International Cooperation in the 21st Century* (New York and Oxford: Oxford University Press, 1999), xxvii–xxxiv.
6. A helpful overview is provided in Ian Shapiro, *The State of Democratic Theory* (Princeton and Oxford: Princeton University Press, 2003).
7. *See also* my short comments on that issue in chapter one, section "Diversity and Democracy."
8. Knut Wicksell, *Finanztheoretische Untersuchungen nebst Darstellung und Kritik des Steuerwesens Schwedens* (Jena: Verlag Gustav Fischer, 1896).
9. James M. Buchanan analyzes some of the major flaws of Wicksell's proposal in: *Public Finance in Democratic Process: Fiscal Institutions and the Individual Choice* (Chapel Hill: University of North Carolina Press, 1967), 116. Despite these critiques, the unanimity rule was discussed by James Buchanan and Gordon Tullock in *The Calculus of Consent: Logical Foundations of Constitutional Democracy* (Ann Arbor: University of Michigan Press, 1962). They argue that, first of all, one has to do an economic calculus which compares cost reductions due to public goods policies with the costs of making the policies. Secondly, one has to take into account each individual's anticipated loss due to the prospect that collective decisions might harm him. The data then show whether or not a good should be provided as a public good. Another proposal for calculating the benefits and losses of public goods policies is presented in James Buchanan, *The Limits of Liberty: Between Anarchy and Leviathan* (Indianapolis, IN: Liberty Fund, 2000), 46–68. On the level of a post-constitutional contract scenario, one could couple membership with participation in a chosen set of public goods and contribution to it. By this method, public goods are artificially transformed into exclusive goods.

10. When reaching unanimity is illusionary and instead the responsibility of politicians for the lives of all citizens must be appealed to, a minimal demand is that the claims of each citizen should have the same weight as the claim of anyone else. Immediately, there is another problem. A central theorem in social choice theory says that even if there were decisive orders of the preferences of individuals, these orders could not be translated into a collective order of preferences. This is a systematic problem that cannot be resolved at this point. Yet, it should be noted that preferences alone cannot be the yard stick for collective decisions over public goods. For an understandable discussion of Arrow's Impossibility Theorem *see* Amartya Sen, "Rationality and Social Choice," in *Rationality and Freedom* (Cambridge, MA, and London, UK: Belknap Press of Harvard University Press, 2002), 261–299. Further problems result from "adaptive preferences." Sometimes the preferences of individuals do not express what they really wish, but are the result of influences and external forces. For the problem of "adaptive preferences" in political theory, *see* Martha C. Nussbaum, *Women and Human Development: The Capabilities Approach* (Cambridge, UK: Cambridge University Press, 2000), 111–166.

11. Bernard Manin argues that it is extremely difficult to reconcile the requirement for unanimity with "the practical necessities of political life." Bernard Manin, "On Legitimacy and Political Deliberation," *Political Theory* 15, no. 3 (August, 1987): 342. Manin provides arguments for the view that instead of expecting unanimous decisions, the process of deliberation itself helps formulate the political will and generates legitimacy.

12. Representative political bodies do not provide a solution to the problems I am discussing, either. Instead, the same systematic problems surface again on the level of representation. Representative individuals are just another group of individuals whose preferences differ as much as the preferences of citizens differ from each other.

13. The complexity of calculations regarding public goods is illustrated in: Richard Epstein, *Bargaining with the State* (Princeton, NJ: Princeton University Press, 1993). Even though Epstein shows sympathy with political liberalism, his proposal implies the idea of minimal state intervention and the strengthening of private property regimes. For Epstein's systematic approach see: Richard A. Epstein, *Takings: Private Property and the Power of Eminent Domain* (Cambridge, MA, and London, UK: Harvard University Press, 1985).

14. This proposal is made by Richard Epstein in *Skepticism and Freedom: A Modern Case for Classical Liberalism* (Chicago: University of Chicago Press, 2003), 40. For further examples *see* Epstein, *Skepticism* and Freedom, 136.

15. Bruce Ackerman and James Fishkin, *Deliberation Day* (New Haven and London: Yale University Press, 2004).

16. Deliberative polling is a preliminary stage for a deliberation day and has been tried out and examined by Fishkin and his colleagues. *See* Ackerman and Fishkin, *Deliberation Day*, 44.

17. Ackerman and Fishkin, *Deliberation Day*, 44.

18. Ackerman and Fishkin, *Deliberation Day*, 55.

19. For a recent contribution that follows the lines of a politics of inclusion without neglecting the need of representative governments *see*: Iris Marion Young, *Inclusion and Democracy* (2nd ed., Oxford: Oxford University Press, 2002).

20. It should be noted that this distinction is different from the much more well-known distinction between "negative" and "positive freedom." For that distinction *see*: Isaiah Berlin, "Two Concepts of Liberty," in *Liberty*, ed. Henry Hardy (Oxford: Oxford University Press, 2002), 166–217.

21. Stephen Holmes and Cass R. Sunstein, *The Cost of Rights: Why Liberty Depends on Taxes* (New York and London: W. W. Norton, 2000).

22. Detailed arguments for and against socioeconomic rights as constitutional rights are provided by Sunstein in: Cass R. Sunstein, *Designing Democracy: What Constitutions Do* (Oxford and New York: Oxford University Press, 2001); *see* esp. chapter 10: "Social and Economic Rights? Lessons from South Africa," 221–237. Sunstein discusses the development of an article of the constitution for South Africa concerning the rights of children to shelter. He considers it a reasonable solution that the constitution did not guarantee an absolute right to public housing, but instead a guarantee that all steps will be done to provide shelter and that programs in favor of this aim get installed. Sunstein, *Designing Democracy*, 231–232.

23. The relationship between freedom, resources, and achievements is explained in Amartya Sen, *Inequality Reexamined* (Oxford: Clarendon Press and Cambridge, MA: Harvard University Press, 1992), 31–37. The differences between functionings, capabilities as sets of functioning achievements, and capabilities sets as capabilities a person actually can choose is summarized in: Amartya Sen, *Development as Freedom* (New York: Knopf, Borzoi Books, 1999), 74–76. Different from Nussbaum, Sen argues that a list of general capabilities cannot be compiled. For this difference, *see* Martha C. Nussbaum, "Capabilities as Fundamental Entitlements: Sen and Social Justice," *Feminist Economics*, 9, no. 2–3 (2003): 33–59.

24. The arguments that are presented in this section rely on the distinction between negative and positive rights. For this distinction see: Alan Gewirth, *The Community of Rights* (Chicago and London: University of Chicago Press, 1996), 33–38. Gewirth stresses that purely positive and purely negative rights are rare; more common are the "mixed cases": "certain prohibited actions and policies

are actually being engaged in and require active intervention to prevent or rectify them." Gewirth, *Rights*, 36. For a discussion of how first-generation rights (political and civil liberties) and second-generation rights (economic and social rights) cling together, *see* Nussbaum, *Women and Human Development*, 96–98.

25. Aristotle, *The Politics* (Harmondsworth: Penguin 1981), VI. 2: 1327 a 40–1327 b 15.

26. For a still recommendable discussion of the model of liberal democracy *see* C. B. MacPherson, *The Life and Times of Liberal Democracy* (Oxford and New York: Oxford University Press, 1977). This study also shows that—to be precise—one has to see that there are many more authors that count as "political liberals," for instance, John Dewey.

27. The tradition of republicanism has its roots in the époque of the Roman Empire; some authors regard the Italian city-states as exemplary realization of republicanism. For an overwiew on political theories of republicanism *see* David Held, *Models of Democracy* (2nd ed. Stanford, CA: Stanford University Press, 1996), 36–69. For a discussion of classic republicanism as a form of government in the Italian city-state *see* Maurizio Viroli, *Machiavelli* (Oxford and New York: Oxford University Press, 1998), 114–147. Viroli explains that a free city-state is one that lives under his own laws and that gives each citizen the freedom to participate in political affairs and political deliberation. Viroli, *Machiavelli*, 126–129.

28. I shall not discuss at this point whether or not civic republicanism really stands the test of time and is acceptable as a program for democracies.

29. *See* Cass Sunstein, *Why Societies Need Dissent* (Cambridge, MA: Harvard University Press, 2003).

30. Jane Jacobs, *The Death and Life of Great American Cities* (New York: Vintage Books 1992), 95ff.

31. I shall expand on this point in chapter 7.

32. In other words, the commitment to public goods is not restricted to the *political policy*, but also comprises *political process*. I borrow the distinction between "political policy" and "political process" from Philip Pettit. As for republican politics, Pettit explains: "The process commitment required public decisions to be taken in a way that tracks the common, recognizable interests of citizens. The policy commitment, as traditional republicans saw it, required public decisions to promote domestic peace and external defence and perhaps other such goods." Philip Pettit, *Republicanism: A Theory of Freedom and Government* (Oxford and New York, 1997), 288. In defending the role of public goods for democracy, I come close to a republican ideal of democracy that—according to Pettit—is encapsulated in the idea of freedom as non-dominion.

7

CONDITIONS OF A REASONABLE PLURALISM

Public goods serve political aims that are intimately related to democracy. Public goods support the generation of the public, they improve conditions of social justice and they serve aims of political self-determination. Having explained all this, two main problems remain. Opponents might agree to the general thesis that public goods are favorable for central goals in democracy, but they might still insist that it is not very likely to achieve these results. The reason is that there might be no chance of finding goods that actually meet both conditions that define a public good. An opponent can argue that there are no goods that meet the conditions of open access and basic availability. In this chapter I shall take up the objection that there might be no goods that meet the open access condition. The second problem will be discussed in the next chapter.

A person who denies the reliability of the open access condition can make the following claim: Even when goods are made available to the public and even when it can be observed that a list of goods have actually become public, this process will not reach a point at which these goods meet conditions of open availability. There will be access barriers that have selective effects. This again, might have several reasons. One of the most important reasons for a situation like that has been of major concern in theories of political liberalism. It says that whenever collective goods are provided, they relate to value systems of those who engage for public goods and of the community that benefits from them. The implication is that each type of good that deserves this name because of its role in a community of people *cannot* be separated from distinct values. This, in turn, means that participation in these goods as well as provision of these goods depend on value commitments. As a consequence, there are invisible walls which actually surround the so-called public goods.

One lesson of studying the history of some of the central public goods is that this reservation really has to be taken seriously. There might be further reasons why public goods cannot be provided to a degree that actually allows each person to participate in that good. Yet, the reservation that comes from political liberalism is crucial because it results from a systematic problem. Health care and education are examples that demonstrate this problem particularly well. Even though these goods have turned into goods that meet the basic availability condition in many areas of the world, they have not become public since they still do not meet the open access condition. Instead, the provision of these goods is guaranteed because religious associations and non-governmental organizations have shown commitment to these goods. And if so: Can we make sure that these organizations refrain from developing access conditions that result in exclusion of individuals who do not share the value commitments of the providers? In order to illustrate this point, I shall start with a story that is situated in Chicago in the 1950s.

In his book *The Lost City: Discovering the Forgotten Virtues of Community in the Chicago of the 1950s*, Alan Ehrenhalt describes the Chicago of half a century ago.[1] His critical discussion takes up issues as controversial as freedom of choice then and now, authoritarianism, and the changing role of the private and the public. His report touches on public goods in a particular way. Ehrenhalt is interested in the relationship between religious communities and the provision of local goods that are open to the public. The following two passages from Ehrenhalt's book will serve as a starting point for the broader question for which Rawls has coined the expression "reasonable pluralism."[2] In mixed societies, citizens are not only confronted with the plurality of worldviews and values. Rather they also have to acknowledge that different worldviews—most of which can be called "reasonable" in some respect—are at stake and provoke conflict. In political philosophy, pluralism has to be accepted as fact and solutions have to be elaborated for resulting conflicts.[3] A particularly strong cause for conflicts results from religious worldviews. Simultaneously, religious communities are among the most important and most enthusiastic providers of education, health care, and cultural goods.

> Our first visit is to St. Nicholas of Tolentine parish, an enclave of white working-class Catholics toward the southwestern edge of the city. . . . A Chicago neighborhood, as late as the 1950s, was a place in which people lived their lives more or less in public, in full view of their neighbors. . . . To live in a bungalow in St. Nick's parish was to live in a place where the walls of one's house did not constitute boundaries, where social life was conducted on the front stoop and in the alley, and where, even inside the house, four or five children in a three-bedroom home made privacy a rare commodity . . . . The parishioners of St. Nick's lived their lives not only through the church but through its subsidiary organizations, the Holy Name Society, the Altar and Rosary–engines of mass neighborhood participation that brought five hundred or more residents of a single neighbourhood to pancake breakfasts at seven o'clock on a weekday morning.[4]

At the core of St. Nick's parish life was, of course, the Holy Mass. But there was another strong pillar—the school.

> Even those in the neighborhood who felt less than comfortable with parish life . . . sent their children to the St. Nick's parish elementary school. . . . Tuition at St. Nick's was virtually free. Each family paid two dollars a month and that covered as many children as the parents wanted to send. Those two dollars bought the educational services of eighteen nuns whose classrooms each contained more than fifty students. To look at a photograph of a St. Nick's classroom in those days is to confront an endless sea of faces, so many that it almost seems like trick photography. The vastness is only accentuated by the uniformity of their appearance: white blouse with red tie and Peter Pan collar for the girls, light blue long-sleeved shirt and navy blue tie for the boys. A child who showed up out of uniform was sent home for the day. . . . Every Friday, most of the children of St. Nick's went to confession, where they admitted disobeying parents, fighting with siblings, using bad words, lying about their homework, occasionally lifting something from a store on Sixty-third Street. . . . And every Sunday morning, at nine o'clock, they would arrive for mass and sit together with members of their school class rather than with their families.[5]

This story is a story of the past and from a special place. Even though religious life and community structures differ from place to place and from time to time, people from different places will be in a position to recall similar memories. Reactions, however, differ. One might mourn the loss of an age in which individuals were embedded in the security of parishes, like St. Nick's, and a well-ordered lifecycle; or one may applaud the end of that time as a gain in terms of liberty and freedom. As for public goods, one thing is apparent: A situation in which not only the school but also kindergartens, care institutions, the hospital, and maybe even public places are under the control of one and the same institution—in the community described by Ehrenhalt, the Catholic Church, although one could just as easily envision a different kind of monopoly—a situation like that cannot provide conditions for a public good in terms of the open access condition.

In this chapter, I wish to question the role of churches and denominations as providers of public goods as part of a broader problem in political philosophy. As a matter of fact, individuals cling to different worldviews. Modern societies and political institutions in particular have to cope with resulting tensions and conflicts. Regarding public schools and health care, tensions include the role of religion. The *first section* of this chapter gives a short overview of the history of education and health care in Europe. It demonstrates the increasing and rather late-coming influence of state institutions and thereby also explains how some goods have been transformed from private goods to welfare goods. In the *second section*, I shall start discussing philosophical perspectives on the relationship between the need for a reasonable pluralism in plural societies and goods that—at first glance—cannot be separated from value issues. Liberalism provides an approach to deal with diversity regarding values and worldviews. I wish to show that liberalism provides a good starting point, but has to be transcended at some point. In the *third section*, I wish to elaborate on a solution that at some point deviates from liberalism but nevertheless shares common ground with liberal approaches to pluralism. It pays tribute to the fact that neither institutions that provide goods nor the institutions themselves can be completely purified from ideas of the good life. Instead of denying value dimensions, a differentiation of three different spheres of values helps provide an alternative approach to argue for a pluralism regarding public goods. In the *fourth section*, I get back to religion. I shall draw some conclusions for the role of religious communities and denominations in providing public goods. I shall also try to give a reply to theologians who wish to strengthen the role of religion in public life. Yet, the remarks on religion are no more than cursory.

HEALTH CARE AND EDUCATION: SOME HISTORICAL REMARKS

With respect to differences in value judgments, it can be argued that health care and public education are among the most controversial goods. As compared to infrastructure or security, the values that are encapsulated in education and in institutions of care transcend the level of instrumental values of practicability and good design. A sketch of some historical facts about these goods may help us understand the issues at stake. This overview can, of course, not give a comprehensive picture; it has to be taken rather for representing some interesting steps in the development of education and health care as public goods.

Roughly speaking, the emergence of health care and education in Europe was marked by four stages. The *first stage* occurred in the middle ages, when education and care for poor people were closely tied to monasteries. Hospitals attached to monasteries and parishes had many functions. They provided refuge for homeless people, aged people, and orphans; they also distributed alms for poor people and for travellers. Guilds and fraternities similarly engaged in good deeds and alms.[6] This stage of religious commitment to poor people cannot be understood without relating it to the overall attitude toward poverty at the time. Poverty was not considered a result of individual failure, but rather an invitation by God to do good deeds. Good deeds, in turn, could ensure access to heaven. In this stage, then, investing in care was an expression of religiously motivated solidarity with poor people. The Franciscans and Dominicans not only showed solidarity with them, they also celebrated them.[7]

This situation changed when the plague of the Black Death came to Europe in the 1340s. As a *second stage* of the development I am describing, in Nuremberg and Cologne, begging was henceforth forbidden. Poverty and misery reached a level that could not be addressed by former means. In the 14th century, municipalities such as Barcelona and Valencia started providing subsidies for churches; taxes were levied on poor people in Sweden and Paris, while in Turin, one could publicly enlist for charity. At this second stage in our history, the picture of cooperation in provision of some goods emerges. In the 16th century, the increase both in population and in poverty reinforced the fear of mass riots. Governments and municipalities stepped in to prevent the worst.

The *third stage* is the enormous growth of private initiatives and charities, as well as the development of systematic approaches by the state to reduce poverty. One precondition for concentrated state intervention was territorial consolidation. States such as Spain, England, and France became stronger by ruling these territories—a process that finally led to the modern nation-state. Although different states exhibited different priorities, public education and public aid were high among them. Already in 1601 in England, poor people had access to aid, while free education came only in the 19th century. In Prussia and France, by contrast, free education preceded relief for poor people.[8] With growing state intervention, private giving also increased. The 18th century became the century of philanthropic organizations. It is impossible here to portray the diversity of these developments. There were numerous societies that focused not only on relief for poor people, but that also strived to reform prisons, improve schools, care for juvenile delinquents, teach programs for better housekeeping (the School of Cookery in London, for example), and train nurses. Care for people in need included public housing programs and welfare programs for infants.

There were also numerous societies that focused on different social aims. Their motives and reasons for committing to social issues were as diverse as those of the institutions providing goods. Philanthropy, as understood in the time of the Enlightenment, was a social act intended to improve society as a whole.[9] One proclaimed aim of the revolutionaries in France was to eradicate poverty. States were interested in social peace, and the churches regarded solving the social issue as an intrinsically valuable endeavor. The historian William B. Cohen concludes that "there was often interaction between private and public spheres in providing aid for poor people, and it is impossible to separate the two."[10]

The *fourth stage* of the development in Europe is the rise of the welfare state. By the end of the 19th century, people began to realize that state intervention was necessary to temper the consequences of industrialization. Research in the social cause led to stunning insights about the gravity of the problem. Simultaneously, governments became increasingly interested in alleviating the conditions of poor people. Combined with a growing optimism about the human ability to transform the environment and the formation of social movement, the groundwork was laid for the extensive welfare states of the second half of the 20th century. Philanthropy and charity organizations either supplement state efforts through established institutions of care and education or respond to still unresolved social issues and needs.

In stepping back from the current situation for a moment and in looking at the cursory remarks on the history of select goods, two things need to be emphasized: *First*, some goods have definitely evolved out of a religious context. This process has been shaped by many factors. The condition of state institutions, the degree of the effectiveness of administrative institutions, the readiness of different institutions to co-operate for a common purpose have all been as important as motivations resulting from political goals and social ideals. So, in fact, this history is much less secular and much less uniform than we might have imagined. This observation is not limited to certain states in Europe. Even though the history of education, e.g., in the United States is even more complicated than in Europe because it is closely intertwined with the history of immigration and its patterns, it is not overstated to say that as for education, religious groups and communities were the most important providers.[11]

Secondly, the growing gap between state and churches was a necessary, but not sufficient, condition for the emergence of public goods in their current form. Competition over local public goods was a good means to increase the diversity and the overall supply. This gap simultaneously allowed for forces that could counterbalance the influence of the political establishment. This struggle has by no means come to an end. The impact of faith-based groups on the delivery of basic services to citizens is a recent example of how far-reaching the influence of churches and religious bodies still is.[12]

To tell the story of institutions of education and care adequately, it is also essential to remind us that cooperation between religious and non-religious institutions is of course not a story of the past. Care for poor and needy members of society has always been and still is part of the religious endeavor to enhance the common good. Religious relief agencies are telling examples, not of a decline of this trend, but of an ambitious international agenda. Religion's support of relief is part of its self-defined public role. The involvement of religious institutions also goes beyond health care and basic education: Religious institutions advocate for higher education, nurseries, and even for infrastructure and environmental goods.[13]

A SOLUTION FROM POLITICAL LIBERALISM

Goods like health care and education have increasingly grown public.[14] The emancipation of these goods from religious contexts is part of the history of liberal societies. Yet, to conclude from this that they have been transformed into neutral goods or that they can be administered on neutral grounds is a false conclusion. The goods mentioned are no value-free zones. Instead, institutions that care for them do so for reasons that in most cases are related to particular value commitments. It is impossible to abstract entirely from the diversity of motives that comprise the commitments to a group of individuals, the ideas about ideals that should be realized in life or simply contributing to a rich civil society.[15] Benefits that spring from education or care are not neutral, either. They support a basically good life of individuals in certain respects.

When shifting to the current situation, it must also be noticed that institutions of education and health care provide occasions for clashes concerning the role of religion and the alleged demands of secularism as well as clashes concerning value questions in a broader sense. Sheer vandalism set aside, it looks as if public goods function as focal points in which the contradictory forces of plural societies play out and crystallize. Disputes over head scarves in public schools in France, legal battles over crucifixes in classrooms in southern Germany, and the list of Supreme Court decisions on the school prayer in the United States are recent examples.[16] To these problems, political liberalism has tried to provide solutions. Two of them can directly be related to our problem. It is the solution that John Rawls labelled the "conditions for a reasonable pluralism" and a reformulation of the idea of "non-integralism" by Rosenblum. I shall discuss both solutions in turn.

John Rawls argues that if societies aim at distributing basic goods and burdens according to principles of justice, individual worldviews have to be handled with care. In particular, individuals are invited to set aside their personal values in public debate. Rawls's proposal must be seen as part of his approach to provide the grounds for a reasonable pluralism in diverse societies. Since his early contributions to political philosophy, John Rawls made proposals for coping with pluralism. It is not overstated to say that the whole program of *Political Liberalism* is built on the acknowledgment of pluralism and dedicated to provide an answer for it. The hope to resolve value conflicts stems from the endowment of individuals with reason. As reasonable beings, individuals can reach reasonable agreement. Yet, the price is an exclusion of doctrines that are comprehensive and value-laden worldviews.[17] When entering the public arena, individuals should leave their values behind and translate their views into sound arguments. From that starting point, reasonable agreement on the duties of political institutions can also be reached.

Appealing as this proposal is, it has some unwelcome consequences. In Rawls's theory of justice, the duties of political institutions are limited to basic constitutional matters and justice.[18] As a further effect, the sphere of the public, that can be shaped by political institutions, shrinks. It is not perfectly consequent when Rawls's theory comprises proposals for education and curricula for schools.[19] Rawls is ready to admit that education is important for socializing pupils as citizens and even argues for "fair equality of opportunity in education."[20] Yet, it is interesting to notice that Rawls does not appear to be *against* public goods. It rather seems as if the severity of value clashes contributes to the view that they cannot be part of the agenda of political liberalism. Rawls's proposal can be interpreted as a contribution to solve methodological problems that surface in demarcating the sphere of politics regarding justice. But it has severe effects on the concept and reality of public goods. Following Rawls, debating a comprehensive list of public goods cannot be part of the political agenda because they do not fit the demands set by public reasoning. They are related to value questions and transcend constitutional essentials in Rawls's view. Instead of engaging in public goods, Rawls's approach leads to the recommendation of respecting the limits of political influence.

A different line of thought in liberalism does not start with demands of justice, but focuses on political institutions. On the institutional level, the demand to respect pluralism can be translated into an institutional guarantee for non-integralism. Political liberals hold the view that individuals should not be forced to comply with a particular worldview that transcends commitments as citizens. According to a definition given by Rosenblum, "integralists want to be able to conduct themselves according to the injunctions of religious law and authority in every sphere of everyday life, and to see their faith mirrored in public life."[21] Non-integralism, instead, demands a separate sphere of public life that is not shaped according to a particular worldview. A clear case of an offense against non-integralism is a close liaison between state and church.[22] From the perspective of political liberals, political institutions should care for non-integralism in supporting and protecting political values in the public.

The crucial question to ask is what non-integralism exactly means as related to public goods. If non-integralism is a reasonable demand: Does this mean that public goods should not be provided by religious bodies? And does non-integralism also include the demand to purify public goods not only from religious values, but from moral values as well? In the remainder of this chapter, I shall argue that non-integralism is the basis for a reasonable pluralism as related to public goods. Yet, instead of demanding to purify public goods from values, a focus on political values helps transcend particular worldviews that are related to public goods. As a consequence, Rawls is right in emphasizing political values. But he overlooks the fact that these values can be attached to public goods as well as to matters of constitutional essentials.

THREE VALUE DIMENSIONS

The problem that goods are not neutral applies to all kinds of public goods. At this point we can widen the view and go back to a general theoretical level. Public goods are not neutral in that they can be protected and built without value commitments. But this does not have to be equalled with another statement about public goods. That statement says that there are no public goods that fulfill the open access condition.

In this chapter I wish to show that neither statement can be reduced to the other.

Many problems have been caused by mixing up three different value dimensions that play a role in public goods regimes. A differentiation, instead, brings us closer to understanding why the conclusion that goods cannot meet the open access condition is *not* correct. In this section, I shall first distinguish three value dimensions that all are related to public goods.[23] Then I shall explain how these value commitments can be settled without opposing basic liberal intuitions.

Regarding public goods, there are three value dimensions that matter. *Firstly*, public goods deliver particular services and benefits. These benefits support a distinct vision of a basically good life. Even though related to life plans as instrumental goods, they are only valuable insofar as they support basic functional capabilities.[24] This first dimension shall be called the dimension of a *functional value*. *Secondly*, providers of goods do so for reasons that might mirror particular value commitments. Motives and reasons are not neutral. Instead, they are related to particular worldviews. I shall call this second dimension the *supporter's value*. *Third*, beneficiaries who profit from public goods cannot strip themselves from their worldviews. Instead, they import their individual commitments to the sphere of public goods. The third value dimension shall be called *imported value*. Each dimension shall be explained in turn.

As for the *functional value*, public goods are valuable insofar as they support individuals in coming into a position of realizing a basically good life. In chapter 5 I have argued that public goods contribute to a particular set of conditions for a basically good life. Yet, this value dimension can be distinguished from individual worldviews and commitments to values in a different sense. The worth of infrastructure, education, environmental goods, health care, and culture cannot be identified with a particular religious commitment, nor do these goods provide answers to meaning-of-life questions. Even though related to a notion of the good life, public goods rather play an instrumental role. They contribute to enhancing living conditions; they do not constitute a good life itself. This is the reason why this value dimension deserves the name "functional value."

As for the *supporter's value*, the provision of public goods usually goes hand in hand with a set of distinct reasons and motives. As it is difficult to examine motives of institutions, a look at motives of individuals, who contribute to public goods, might help understand the diversity of motivational values. In a recent contribution on voluntarism in America, Robert S. Ogilvie demonstrates the diversity of motives that individuals report when—for instance—caring for the homeless people of New York. Sometimes, individuals work voluntarily for social services because they just wish to "give something back" to the community; sometimes, experiences in community projects help people to grow beyond what they expected from themselves; sometimes they do so for reasons of humanity or for explicitly religious motives.[25] In short, the reasons why individuals—and presupposed also institutions—contribute to goods vary. And so do value commitments. People and individuals have engaged in the establishment of those goods listed above for a wide range of different reasons. Religious motives and motivation which relates to a particular worldview might be among these reasons.

As for *imported values*, those who partake in education or in the benefits from health care do not strip themselves of their value commitments before entering the realm of those institutions. Even though individuals might be in a position to distinguish between private and public goods, they cannot get rid of their commitments completely when they participate in public goods. Those who benefit from public transport or from public space do not come as persons who have been stripped of their value commitments. Rather, they enter the public realm as persons with a distinct set of values. Even though it is hard to imagine that individuals get rid of their value systems, it might be sensible to ask them not to use the public realm to live their value commitments.[26]

After having explained how value commitments have to be differentiated, I shall now ask whether political liberalism provides an answer to the challenges that result from diversity in values. Opinions on what education has to achieve and how infrastructure must work vary. So do opinions on the whole range of public goods. There is no coherent approach that explains the role of the media, of institutions of care, and of environmental goods in enhancing living conditions. In order to defend the possibility that access conditions do not have to be combined with value commitments, two steps are necessary. *First*, it is necessary to recall the distinction between different value commitments that are related to public goods. None of them contributes to something like an inherent value of a public good. Each of them can be separated from the content and the structure of a public good. *Secondly*, political liberalism does not say that there are *no* values at all involved in political practices and in the theoretical framework of democracy. Instead, it says that value commitments should not transcend the boundaries of political values. As for public goods, the commitment to political values provides the critical test of whether or not a value commitment can be tolerated.

Most important are the second and third value dimension. As for the second value dimension, the *supporter's value*, instead of trying to build a wall between secular and religiously motivated groups that contribute to public goods and instead of restricting the provision of public goods to political institutions alone, liberalism gives another clue to coping with diversity in motives. It would be a mistake to interpret political liberalism as demanding the political arena and political institutions to be value-free zones. As Rawls has made particularly clear in his later writings, the realm of politics includes a particular set of "political values."[27] A political conception of liberalism does not understand the political sphere as a value-free zone, but as restricted to political values alone. In turn, supporters of public goods must be asked whether or not they subscribe to social justice as social inclusion and therefore are ready to provide access conditions that are not restricted to select individuals.

As for the third value dimension, the *imported value*, those who benefit from public goods also will import their worldviews. Instead of demanding neutrality in that respect and instead of primarily emphasizing potential conflicts, public goods can also provide a realm for civilized exchange of different value commitments. The condition that has to be met is something similar to the concept of sustainability that applies to common pool resources. Imported values are no problem as long as they do not have aversive effects on the capacity of a good to deliver its benefits for individuals who will wish to profit from it in the future. Within a more optimistic scenario, one might also think that public goods offer a realm within which individuals have plenty occasions to learn from each other and to practice tolerance.[28]

This brings us back to the question of which role religion and communities that adhere to a distinct set of values can actually play in public goods. Some answers have already been given. If religious bodies subscribe to the political ideal of free access to all citizens, they should be free to commit themselves to the provision of public goods. From these debates, another question has to be distinguished. It is the question whether or not religious values should be imported into the realm of the public. At the end of this chapter I wish to give voice to theologians who present their idea of how the public realm could be filled with religious life. Even though these perspectives can only be dealt with cursorily, they will introduce some ideas about the relation between public goods and religion.

A VOID IN THE PUBLIC SQUARE

From the perspective of some theologians, Western societies have undergone a dramatic change in recent decades. As a side effect of primarily focusing on individual conceptions of the good life, something like a void has been generated in the midst of our societies. It has been generated unintentionally. Yet, it should not be accepted too easily—too big is the danger that this void can be utilized by forces that endanger tolerance and diversity.

The emerging void can be described in different ways. Some theologians in particular complain of "a silencing of religion in the public square. What has rushed in to fill the void is not noble discussions about principles of justice which have been extracted in Rawlsian fashion from the consensus populi. For nobody *cares about* principles of justice thus obtained. What has rushed in to fill the void is mainly considerations of economic self-interest, of privatism, and of nationalism. These today dominate our discourse in the public square. For people do genuinely care about their own economic well-being, they do genuinely care about protecting their private lives, and many of them do genuinely care about their nation."[29] This is the diagnosis Nicholas Wolterstorff offers in his critical discussion of political liberalism.[30] Other theologians call more directly for a reconsideration of the public role of religion.[31] Part of this claim is not to overcharge the idea of separation between state and church. Jean B. Elshtain criticizes this overcharging as *liberal monism*[32] and demands a more capacious liberalism. The overcharging leads to a view according to which not only a properly secular state is asked for, but also "a thoroughly secularised society—one stripped of any and all public markers and reminders of religion."[33] This does not only lead to the taming of an important voice in democracies, but also to a "built-in animus against the determination by religious denominations to sustain their own network of schools, welfare provision, political advocacy, and so on."[34]—Something that could indeed be catastrophic for those who need these benefits.

Even if the public role of religion is regarded more cautiously,[35] it can be argued that the relation between the public and the private sphere of life have been changing in contemporary societies. In his study on the historical roots of civil society, Adam B. Seligman argues that a more or less exclusive reliance on rights undermines affective solidarity in liberal societies. Seligman argues "that ethical solidarity . . . realized or attained through the universalization of citizenship (i.e., the endowment of all with universal rights), voids the area of shared public (and in the 18th century perforce ethical) space of any value attributes independent of the individuals inhabiting that space."[36] To avoid a misunderstanding, it must be added that this critique is not intended to ask for another basis than legal rights. Instead, it aims at explaining some recent developments, in particular "that the realm of shared public space, within which the citizen is constituted, has itself disappeared."[37] This is quite a harsh diagnosis. It becomes more understandable when we take a closer look at what Seligman has in mind.

Individuals have an appearance in the public only as "generalized universals. . . . "It is precisely in these terms that we are to understand 'the right to wear fur' or even 'women's reproductive rights.' None of these are citizen rights. They are, rather, private passions and interests projected into the public arena in terms of rights. . . . In lieu of the public the private is projected into the public arena, is made public, in an attempt to reconstitute itself through its representation in that sphere."[38] The ultimate reason for this development is not that the private is overrated, nor is it the case "that the public space lacks value, but that it lacks autonomous value in and of itself."[39]

The picture that these authors draw of liberal societies today, illustrating how far-reaching societies have changed their outlook, is quite the opposite from the description given at the beginning of this chapter. Instead of being integrated into a more or less closed life-world, individuals now suffer from a loss of public life. It would be another project to argue for the impact that public goods can have on that situation. Yet, at first sight, public goods can be considered to have some positive effects on the situation without falling back behind liberal ideals. A certain degree of public goods might help remedy the impression of "the void" within our Western societies.

Public goods can provide a realm that can be shared by individuals with different worldviews. A precondition for this possibility is the differentiation of values in terms of functional values, supporter's values and imported values. Under this condition, public goods can provide a layer of appreciable, but nevertheless secular goods within societies that are committed to pluralism. If all participants are ready to accept the services of public goods, there might even be less need to overrun the public space with religious or other fundamentally important value commitments.

TOWARDS DIVERSITY

According to the view outlined in this chapter, pluralism does not result from a shared set of commitments that remains after individuals have stripped themselves of their personal value commitments that are part of their reasonable worldviews. Pluralism in terms of public goods rather acknowledges diversity in values that are related to public goods. In distinguishing three value dimensions, proposals have been elaborated to reconcile the claim that public goods are not neutral items with the claim that they are still not exclusive.

There is a further implication. The argumentation does not express the view that governments are best suited to provide public goods—e.g., because they can play a neutral role. Instead, both state institutions and civil society have to keep a watch on institutions that contribute to public goods to make sure that political values are respected in providing public goods. In order to be in the position of exercising mutual control, each providing institution must be hindered from playing the role of monopolies. In plural societies, diversity of public goods is an appropriate means to satisfy the needs and wishes of a plural society.

NOTES

1. Alan Ehrenhalt, *The Lost City: Discovering the Forgotten Virtues of Community in the Chicago of the 1950s* (New York: Basic Books, 1995).

2. For Rawls's interpretation of "reasonable pluralism" and "reasonable comprehensive doctrines" *see* John Rawls, *Political Liberalism* (New York: Columbia University Press, 1996), 58–66.

3. According to Rawls, a reasonable pluralism is a feature of democratic public culture. It is achieved best by means of limiting the influence of reasonable comprehensive doctrines, that all claim truth for themselves, on political issues. He says that "we are to recognize the practical impossibility of reaching reasonable and workable political agreement in judgment on the truth of comprehensive doctrines, especially an agreement that might serve the political purpose, say, of achieving peace and concord in a society characterized by religious and philosophical differences." Rawls, *Political Liberalism*, 63.

4. Ehrenhalt, *The Lost City*, 28–30.

5. Ehrenhalt, *The Lost City*, 127–128.

6. In this brief overview, I draw on William B. Cohen, "Epilogue: The European Comparison," in *Charity, Philanthropy, and Civility in American History*, ed. Lawrence J. Friedman and Mark D. McGarvie (Cambridge: Cambridge University Press, 2003), 385–412. For a discussion of the history of health care and education in Europe and in the United States *see* also Peter Lindert, *Growing Public: Social Spending and Economic Growth since the Eighteenth Century, Vol. I: The Story* (Cambridge: Cambridge University Press, 2004). In a second volume, Lindert's study also provides statistics and empirical data on the growth of health care and education in the last century.

7. Cohen, *The European Comparison*, 386–388.

8. Cohen, *The European Comparison*, 399.

9. Cohen, *The European Comparison*, 396.

10. Cohen, *The European Comparison*, 398.

11. For the role of voluntary associations and religious groups in providing club goods see Jason Kaufman, *For the Common Good? American Civic Life and the Golden Age of Fraternity* (Oxford and New York: Oxford University Press, 2002). In Part II on "Competitive Voluntarism and American Political Development" (85–162), Kaufman gives a detailed picture of "competitive associationalism" that reached its peak in the United States in the late 19th century. Kaufman argues that different from Europe, American associations lacked a professional surveillance and unifiying forces so that "the associational movement of the postbellum era accentuated the lines that divide and hardened Americans' resistance to collectivization of risks and resources. As a result, America missed its primary opportunity to join western Europe in the adoption of people-friendly social policies." Kaufmann, *Common Good*, 198.

12. For a discussion of the current situation and a reassessment of its diversity see Robert Wuthnow, *Saving America? Faith-Based Services and the*

Future of Civil Society (Princeton, NJ: Princeton University Press, 2004). I shall not get deeper into the debate on faith-based services; I think that debate is complicated and should be led on separate grounds.

13. Rhys H. Williams demonstrates that religion and religious communities can provide natural bases for social movement activism. See Rhys H. Williams, "Religious Social Movement in the Public Sphere: Organization, Ideology, and Activism," in *Handbook of the Sociology of Religion*, ed. Michele Dilon (Cambridge: Cambridge University Press, 2003), 315–330.

14. "Growing Public" is the telling title of Peter H. Lindert's comparative study on the history of social spending. Lindert gives a detailed picture of social spending in Europe before 1880 and discusses the rise of public schooling. It is not possible to summarize his findings in few words. Of particular importance for the issues of this chapter is the insight that diversity in religion, voting rights and the rise of public schooling were intertwined. "Democracy and voting outperformed religion as directly competing influences on schooling. . . . Still, religious diversity might have been a historical *parent* rather than a competitor, of democracy as an influence on schooling. Most countries with diverse religions in the 19th century had reached an uneasy balance that often guaranteed freedoms of religion and local political voice. The whole nexus of relative tolerance helped both democracy and schooling to blossom in the 19th century, when the economic demand for schooling was becoming obvious. Religious diversity, democracy, and schooling were probably intertwined." Lindert, *Growing Public*, 110. Italics by Lindert.

15. The diversity of motives is restated in Kaufman's study on associationalism in the history of the United States. For immigrants, ethnicity was an important pattern of association. *See* Kaufman, *Common Good*.

16. A discussion of the "German scarf affair" from the perspective of political philosophy is provided by Seyla Benhabib in: *The Rights of Others: Aliens, Residents, and Citizens* (Cambridge, UK: Cambridge University Press, 2004), 198–202.

17. "Reasonable comprehensive doctrines" have three special properties: They cover major religious, philosophical, and moral aspects of human life in a more or less consistent and coherent manner. Theoretical and practical reason are used in their formulation. And—even though not necessarily fixed and unchanged—they draw upon a tradition of thought and doctrine. *See* Rawls, *Political Liberalism*, 59.

18. Rawls, *Political Liberalism*, 227–230. For a helpful discussion of this limitation see Charles Larmore, "Public Reason," in *The Cambridge Companion to Rawls*, ed. Samuel Freeman (Cambridge, UK: Cambridge University Press, 2002), 380–384.

19. "[Political liberalism] will ask that children's education include such things as knowledge of their constitutional and civic rights so that, for example, they know that liberty of conscience exists in their society and that apostasy is not a legal crime, all this to insure that their continued membership when they come of age is not based simply on ignorance of their basic rights or fear of punishment for offenses that do not exist. Moreover, their education should also prepare them to be fully cooperating members of society and enable them to be self-supporting; it should also encourage the political virtues so that they want to honor the fair terms of social cooperation in their relations with the rest of society." Rawls, *Political Liberalism*, 199.

20. Rawls, *Political Liberalism*, 184. The rationale Rawls gives for supporting public education is that "society's concern with their education lies in their role as future citizens." Rawls, *Political Liberalism*, 200.

21. Nancy L. Rosenblum, *Membership & Morals: The Personal Uses of Pluralism in America* (Princeton, NJ: Princeton University Press, 1998), 15.

22. Whether or not modern states really have reached a position in which religion is separated from political matters and whether or not it is possible at all to purify public life from religious demands, is a difficult question. A discussion of this issue goes beyond the aim of this chapter. Neither will I discuss the difficulty to separate a sphere of life in which religious and moral values are situated from civil interests. As a philosophical approach that illustrates the difficulties in demarcating that line, *see* John Locke, *A Letter Concerning Toleration* (New York: Prometheus Books, 1990), 18ff.

23. I shall employ "value" in its very wide sense as something that is regarded desirable. In my view, value commitments always are related to particular perspectives.

24. For the underlying arguments, *see* chapter 5.

25. Robert S. Ogilvie, *Voluntarism, Community Life, and the American Ethic* (Bloomington and Indianapolis: Indiana University Press, 2004).

26. Yet, it also should be noted that to ask for hiding private value commitments cuts both ways. On the one hand, if the rights to freedom of speech and to religious freedom are taken seriously, public goods cannot be exempt from these regulations. Each person should have the right to express their worldview in the public. No one should be forced to comply with value standards that contradict his or her personal value commitments. On the other hand, public goods belong to the public realm. In that realm, laws and regulations different from rules regulating the private sphere of life are effective. For an example in case, see Winnifred Fallers Sullivan, *The Impossibility of Religious Freedom* (Princeton and Oxford: Princeton University Press, 2005). Sullivan discusses the implications of American laws on freedom of religion. Her study focuses

on a trial about expression of religious worldviews within the boundaries of a cemetery.

27. For the content of "political values" in Rawls *see* Rawls, *Political Liberalism*, 238ff.

28. At this point, my approach comes close to Michael J. Sandel's recent discussion of civic republicanism as a proposal for a public philosophy that has the ability to strengthen political community. "The republican tradition long viewed the public realm not only as a place of common provision but also as a setting for civic education. The public character of the common school, for example, consisted not only in its financing but also in its teaching; ideally at least, it was a place where children of all classes would mix and learn the habits of democratic citizenship. Even municipal parks and playgrounds were once seen not only as places of recreation but also as sites for the promotion of civic identity, neighborliness, and community." Michael J. Sandel, *Democracy's Discontent: America in Search of a Public Philosophy* (Cambridge, MA, and London, UK: Belknap Press of Harvard University Press, 1996), 332. Unlike Sandel, I do not mean to imply that public goods incorporate community values.

29. Nicholas Woltersdorf, "Why We Should Reject What Liberalism Tells Us about Speaking and Acting in Public for Religious Reasons," in *Religion and Contemporary Liberalism*, ed. Paul J. Weithman (Notre Dame: University of Notre Dame Press, 1997), 177. Italics by Woltersdorf.

30. It has to be added that the development Woltersdorf describes does not result from liberalism per se, but from a particular widespread interpretation of it, that Woltersdorf calls "the separation view." It says that "the government is to do nothing to advance or hinder any religion." Woltersdorf, *Why We Should Reject*, 165. An alternative, which liberals do not take seriously, is a view according to which all religions should be treated "impartially."

31. For a proposal concerning a comprehensive public role of religion, *see* José Casanova, *Public Religions in the Modern World* (Chicago and London: University of Chicago Press, 1994).

32. "What has merged as a hallmark of liberal political philosophy is a position I call liberal monism, by which is meant the view that all institutions internal to a democratic society must conform to a single authority principle (one person, one vote, or some such); a single standard of what counts as reason and deliberation (here Mill and later Millians); and a single vocabulary of political discussion (John Rawls). Democracy is defined in such a way that religion must be kept marginalized." Jean Bethke Elshtain, "The Liberal Social Contract and the Privatization of Religion," in *Religion as a Public Good: Jews and Other Americans on Religion in the Public Square*, ed. Alan Mittleman (Lanham, MD: Rowman & Littlefield, 2003), 20.

33. Elshtain, *The Liberal Social Contract*, 19.

34. Elshtain, *The Liberal Social Contract*, 19.

35. Martin E. Marty and Jonathan Moore argue for religion in publicly funded primary and secondary education. One of the main arguments is the need to learn about religion, because "in the midst of global, national, and local change affecting worldviews and public action, religion is too widespread and too deep a phenomenon *not* to be reckoned with in primary or at least secondary schools and thereafter, no matter under what aegis or auspices." Martin E. Marty with Jonathan Moore, *Education, Religion, and the Common Good: Advancing a Distinctly American Conversation about Religion's Role in Our Shared Life* (San Francisco: Jossey-Bass, 2000), 139.

36. Adam B. Seligman, *The Idea of Civil Society* (Princeton, NJ: Princeton University Press, 1992), 132.

37. Seligman, *Civil Society*, 133.

38. Seligman, *Civil Society*, 134.

39. Seligman, *Civil Society*, 135.

8

A REPLY TO LIBERTARIANS

In this chapter I shall confront a further line of critique. It relates to the basic availability condition and some of its consequences. An opponent might accept the theoretical approach to public goods which has been developed so far, but might nevertheless be much more interested in the aspect of supply than in the effects of public goods on societies. She might go as far as to say that taking into account the supply problem outweighs the benefits that can be expected. For providing beneficiaries with, e.g., a basic level of health care, education, or environmental goods, political institutions need to take care of public finance. Regulation in favor of public goods and management of public goods become necessary, too. In fact, this results in two types of costs for citizens: taxes and unfreedom. When these costs are taken into account, providing public good can no longer be justified. The reason is that benefits and costs have to be balanced out against each other. As for public goods, this calculus does not lead to a positive outcome. Especially when the costs in terms of unfreedom are taken seriously, even the principle of social justice that was defended as a principle of fairness cannot be upheld.

This is an important objection. But it relies on premises that must be called into question. In particular, it mixes up two different lines of thought. In analyzing argumentative strategies of opponents to public goods policies, empirical arguments which draw on negative side effects of intervention and regulation can be distinguished from philosophical arguments that draw on ideas of liberty and freedom. In this chapter I shall argue that a libertarian view derives its persuasive power at least to some degree from the practice of presenting both groups of arguments as interconnected. Is there anyone who will not be convinced that "big governments" damage the common good if the attention is drawn to the costly side effect of vast bureaucracies and inflexible structures? Yet, this empirical argument must be separated from the normative points that certain practices have to be classified as infringements on individual liberties. Whether or not regulation is regarded as infringement on freedom or as a chance to shape a common environment has to be decided on separate grounds.

Before getting started, I should give a more precise description of the opponents I have in mind. Reservations against regulatory and interventionist practices have been articulated most forcefully by a group of philosophers called libertarians. Libertarians argue in favor of individual liberties and oppose government actions to promote either equality or a distinct social order. More specifically, libertarianism defends the rights of self-ownership and, by extension, places emphasis on the right of private ownership of material resources and property. Libertarian approaches do not only argue for minimal governmental structures, they also oppose governmental practices that are classified as interventionist. Advocates of a strict libertarian point of view oppose a regulatory framework and any form of taxation in favor of a laissez-faire economic system.

Libertarian arguments are not restricted to the philosophy of libertarianism, but have become part of political ideas about the role of government as well. Strictly speaking, they oppose welfare goods. But indirectly, their arguments also are important for public goods. Even though I have not provided an approach to a framework that is needed for organizing public goods, some involvement of political institutions is necessary. Therefore, I shall also discuss what the account of public goods that has been discussed in this volume does and does not imply.

This chapter is organized as follows. I shall *first* give a more concrete picture of the kind of background institutions that actually are needed when governments support public goods. This provides the backdrop against which arguments against libertarian reservations can be discussed. As a *second* step, I wish to propose a fourfold scheme of arguments that draws on the distinction between empirical and normative arguments and the distinction between "interventionist practices" and "big governments." *Empirical arguments* rely on an assessment of observable and calculable side effects of policies; *normative arguments* instead focus on the category of freedom. The arguments from *interventionist practices* focus on the impact of regulatory frameworks on the lives of citizens and on the realm of private enterprises; the arguments from *big government* instead focus on the need for state institutions that provide the background conditions for public goods and administer them. Each of them can be combined with each other so that a fourfold scheme emerges.

After having discussed it step by step, a second layer of the debate reveals itself. A final section does not provide the argument that it is *not* the rejection of interventionist practices which provides the most fundamental rationale against public goods, *nor* is it the need for institutional background arrangements. Libertarian reservations rather work with implicit assumptions about the capacities of markets and a corresponding misinterpretation of the capacities of political institutions.

GOVERNMENTAL PRACTICES INVOLVED IN PUBLIC GOODS REGIMES

Due to the variety of public goods, the analysis has to focus on some core factors that are involved when governments in economically developed democratic states support public goods. It is helpful to first mention what public goods regimes do *not* imply. In democracies, public goods are *not* goods which are owned by states, nor will the means of production normally be state-owned. After the fall of the Soviet Union and the breakdown of the economies of former communist countries in Eastern Europe and elsewhere, state-ownership does not appear to be a convincing idea. Instead, public goods can be supported by public finance to some degree and will need a regulatory framework that helps sustain them.

Sometimes, public goods are identified as goods that are financed by means of public finance. Even though public goods have primarily been a matter of concern in financial studies, the identification of public goods as publicly financed goods cannot be derived from this discussion. Financial experts succeeded in demonstrating that public goods cannot easily be integrated into market structures. Support for public goods through public finance is necessary because otherwise public goods would either not be produced at all or not to a sufficient degree.[1] But still, it has nowhere been said that the costs of public goods have to be fully covered by means of public finance.[2] In many cases, mixed regimes imply the third sector and an involvement of the private sector as well as tax schemes.

When goods such as security, infrastructure, environmental goods, education, health care, and cultural institutions are supported by means of public finance, their administration does not have to lie in the hands of political institutions or governments. An involvement of political institutions in the administration of public goods cannot be equated with a situation in which those institutions fully cover the managerial demands. Instead, a situation in which political involvement is restricted to the formulation of core guidelines and their enforcement is—in some cases—more suitable to the functions of public goods as connectivity goods and as identification goods. Institutions of education, institutions of health care, even institutions for protection of the environment and infrastructure—all these public goods can be realized by institutions on various levels that are autonomous up to a certain degree.[3]

Consequently, political commitment to public goods does not amount to a comprehensive management of public goods or to anything close to a planned economy. However, the sustenance of public goods still includes practices that are highly controversial from a libertarian perspective. Legislation and policies of regulation in favor of public goods are—from a libertarian point of view—regarded as unwelcome interventions into the sphere of economy and into the private sphere of life of citizens.

AN ANALYSIS OF ARGUMENTS

Arguments and reservations about an active support for public goods are widespread—both in everyday life and in academic thinking. Critical assessments of state involvement in public goods policies are either centered on what these practices entail for the institutions themselves or on the impact of the practices on the economy. The main arguments are that if regulation becomes necessary, governmental structures necessarily grow; the impact on the economy is by and large also considered as a negative one. These are two sides of the same problem; they are, however, separable. In addition to distinguishing arguments against "big government" from arguments against intervention into the private sphere of life, normative arguments can be distinguished from empirical arguments. My discussion will follow this fourfold scheme.

I shall start with arguments against "big government" as empirical arguments and shall then proceed to normative arguments against "big government." I shall then discuss the arguments against intrusion into the economic sphere and again will first give the empirical and then the normative arguments. The discussion is certainly not exhaustive, and it is not intended to be so. It rather aims at presenting and discussing a systematic outline of the structure of libertarian arguments against public goods.

EMPIRICAL ARGUMENTS AGAINST "BIG GOVERNMENT"

Arguments that are frequently brought forward against "big governments" address shortfalls in economic terms. If governmental institutions are involved in the management of a wide range of public goods, a vast administrative system becomes necessary. Tax systems must be developed, implemented, and constantly adjusted to changing circumstances. Legal and juridical systems are needed to develop guidelines for particular goods. Law enforcement, too, will be a costly enterprise. In addition, efficiency is not very likely in vast bureaucracies of the public sector.[4] As institutions that do not have to obey the market laws, public institutions are particularly prone to what Baghwati has called "DUPs." DUPs are "directly unproductive profit-seeking activities" that are supposed to abound in bureaucracies.[5]

Although there is no reason to underestimate resulting problems, this is not an argument against public goods supporting practices, but against bad implementation of necessary procedures. Instead of regarding the problems as matters of principle, they should be regarded as flaws of existing systems. Bad structures can be improved. Joseph E. Stiglitz makes the proposal that crucial factors which ameliorate public administrations can be introduced artificially in public goods regimes.[6] An amelioration of management structures can be achieved through incentives for best performances and by stimulating the competition in a reasonable way. In addition, the economic advantages of private administration still have to be proven. Recent studies on the Health Care System in the United States reveal inefficiencies that possibly could have been avoided in a system that would be administered publicly.[7]

NORMATIVE ARGUMENTS AGAINST "BIG GOVERNMENT"

More convincing are arguments against "big government" that imply normative considerations. At the core of these arguments lies a question that points to a dilemma: How can governments be active without also being paternalistic in their practices? If policies aim at the provision or sustenance of public goods, these practices also infringe upon the private sphere of citizens. Most obviously, tax payments will be required. From a libertarian point of view, to justify this infringement on the private property of citizens is a delicate matter. If property rights can be classified as basic entitlements, taxes can generally be regarded as undue "takings."[8] Since compensation for these takings consists in benefits that not all citizens will at all times partake in, this libertarian reservation appears to hit a central point. To understand this point, it is necessary to go a little deeper into the philosophical idea of property rights.

One version of contractualism says that basic political institutions are justified by a basic contract that all members of a future society agree upon. This contract contains the commitment to give up natural rights in favor of rights that will be protected by a political body. Libertarians agree that security is among the most basic goods citizens agree upon; this implies the right of private property. As a consequence, the right of private property is the foundation of the whole edifice of political institutions and a well-ordered society.[9] Yet, for contractual arguments, almost everything depends on the initial scenario and the choice of relevant parameters.[10] Property rights do not even have to enter the initial scenario at all. Rawls's theory of justice, for instance, starts with an original position that leads to decisive ideas about politics without introducing prior rights at all; the two interests of persons to realize a life plan and a sense of justice, combined with a set of primary goods, suffices for justifying basic principles within a well-ordered society.[11]

My point here is not that different scenarios lead to different outcomes. My point is rather that libertarian ideas about the priority of rights of private property that trump the right to participate in public goods are not self-evident. It relies on premises that already state the priority of property rights. Instead of relying on the right of private property as a natural right, it is convincing to argue that the right of private property is part of a system of institutions and conventions within the realm of political institutions.[12] In *The Cost of Rights: Why Liberty Depends on Taxes*, Stephen Holmes and Cass R. Sunstein argue that property rights are in a line with further rights in that they cannot exist without an active protection by political institutions. This, in turn, presupposes the background of public finance.[13] In short, the idea that public spending for public goods necessarily infringes upon a prior right of private property has to be criticized. This does not imply that "takings" in favor of public goods are necessarily justified. But it implies that financial support for public goods in terms of public finance does not necessarily infringe on another prior right of citizens.

EMPIRICAL ARGUMENTS AGAINST INTERVENTION

According to libertarian ideas about political institutions, some intermediary public goods are necessary because they guarantee the security of citizens. Yet, political institutions should refrain from providing a comprehensive list of final public goods.[14] One central rationale for this recommendation is that policies that accompany the provision of final public goods have to be regarded as non-desirable intrusions into the sphere of industrial production. Intervention has distorting effects on the performance of the private sector. Economics has provided the fundamental rationale for this reservation. The basic mechanisms of the market sphere can only unfold under conditions that do not react to external forces. Once market mechanisms unfold, they guarantee the efficiency of the system as a whole. Resources will be allocated where they are needed. Consumers will be in a position to satisfy their desires to optimal prices. Under conditions of unconstrained performances of a market economy, outcomes are optimal.[15]

This picture relies on some idealizations as economists would be at ease to admit. But in criticizing libertarian reservations against public goods, two idealizations which economists do usually not take into account, are of particular importance. The libertarian assessment of public goods policies as an intrusion into the private sphere of the market and its detrimental effects relies on a certain idealization of the market sphere that has to be criticized. *First*, markets do not necessarily ameliorate the situation of all participants to the same degree. Amartya Sen explains that redistributional effects are only implied in the very minimal sense that nobody will be worse off after having participated in the voluntary exchange processes in the market sphere. Initial endowments, however, will not be corrected.[16] Those who do not have the means to participate right from the beginning will not only *not* profit from the system, but also be excluded from the wealth-enhancing effects. Huge income gaps and growing poverty rates are not only a burden for societies; they also have an impact on the development of human skills and therefore indirectly on the market itself.[17] Investment in public goods, instead, can diminish side effects of markets that cannot be repaired within the market itself.

Secondly, the allegedly detrimental effects of intervention cannot be presupposed as a general fact. Instead, markets appear to need intervention and regulation. Instead of criticizing negative side effects, it should be noted that markets themselves need a framework of regulation. Obvious examples are anti-fraud legislation and the enforcement of quality standards.[18] Yet, the argument goes beyond regulation that focuses on the enhancement of market structures. As I have already argued in chapter 3, public goods also have market-supporting effects. Empirically, most welfare states are doing quite well in terms of economic performance—even though they need vast regulatory schemes to cope with the provision of some welfare goods.[19]

In short, arguments against public goods are not well founded, if they rely on the more general argument that intrusion into the private sphere necessarily produces economically detrimental side effects. Instead, a reliable empirical statement on negative side effects must consider both sides to the coin: the effects of subsidies and regulation on industries and the effects of public goods policies on industrial performances. A general opposition towards public goods and necessary background conditions is not justified on the grounds of objecting "intrusion" into the private sector.

NORMATIVE ARGUMENTS AGAINST INTERVENTION

A final group of libertarian reservations comprises normative arguments against intrusion into the private sphere. A common normative objection against regulation stigmatizes regulation as infringement upon the freedom of individuals. People should be free to make their own choices and there is no justification for depriving people of doing so in their most private sphere of life, namely the decisions about investments and goods one wishes to acquire.[20] Milton and Rose Friedman have given expression to that libertarian critique when they say: "When you vote daily in the supermarket, you get precisely what you voted for, and so does everyone else. The ballot box produces conformity without unanimity; the marketplace unanimity without conformity. That is why it is desirable to use the ballot box, so far as possible, only for those decisions where conformity is essential."[21] Not only is the freedom to choose, but also the freedom to actively participate in the market sphere at stake. People should be free to make contracts and entrepreneurs should be free to set up enterprises.[22] A national prescription of a certain range of goods, on the contrary, hinders people from unfolding as free beings.

In recent years, the concept of freedom and its relation to both effective well-being and to political institutions has been debated intensely in political philosophy.[23] Identifying freedom with freedom of choice can be regarded as too limited a view of human freedom. As Martha Nussbaum argues in her contributions to political philosophy, the freedom to lead a life according to one's own wishes and life plan relies on a whole range of preconditions.[24] People cannot realize their plans without being in a position to make use of central functional capabilities; the realization of these capabilities, again, presupposes a set of conditions that can to some degree be covered by public goods. Providing people with goods which are essential for training the capacities of leading a good life does not prevent people from making a choice. Rather it makes people free to choose and to realize a good life. In short, the provision of public goods does not have to be interpreted as a limitation of freedom; it rather has to be regarded as an enabling condition for individual freedom. Instead of condemning intrusion in the economic sphere in general, it is necessary to distinguish between goods that should be available as a precondition for being in a position to choose and goods that individuals should be free to choose according to individual preferences. Some specific freedom-enhancing goods have to be protected by political means; other goods are best placed within the market sphere.

The impact of public goods policies on freedom also has to be addressed from an altogether different perspective. It is a long tradition in philosophy to understand freedom in terms of a voluntary acceptance of rules and guidelines to which one subordinates one's own wishes. Freedom in that sense is linked to concepts of political self-determination.[25] The model of self-determination applies to individuals as well as to political communities. It has a special meaning in the context of discussing public goods. What the idea of "freedom of choice" does not take into account is that we live in a dense network of causal chains and networks that determine our living conditions. To be free cannot realistically amount to the view that we are free to live without reasonable solutions as for scarce common resources. Even if people were free to buy whatever the market offers, compromises would still be necessary regarding shared living conditions. Against that background, regulation in favor of public goods can amount to taking the chance not to be determined, but to participate in political decisions on common resources to live well.

A final comment goes back to the freedom-of-choice argument. Even though forces of a market-driven economy do not necessarily enhance the provision of public goods and, in fact, can be averse to it, it must also be considered that an unregulated market in the end also endangers freedom of choice. Markets generate selections of goods that fit the structure of demand and supply. Public goods are not missed on that list because they are not desired. There is a demand for public goods, otherwise no one would care about them. But they are endangered through expanding private-property regimes and markets. So, even if one does not agree with conceptions of freedom that emphasize the freedom-enhancing effects of public goods, it can still be argued that the selective mechanisms of markets tend to diminish this kind of goods and therefore severely limits freedom in terms of freedom of choice. If some goods are no longer available, this is a setback for the range of choices.

AGAINST A FOLK THEOREM

An analysis that distinguishes between normative and empirical arguments and between arguments against "big government" and against intrusion into the private sphere can counter libertarian arguments on two different levels. As for empirical arguments, it does not suffice to point out negative side effects of public goods policies. Instead, a reliable judgment about economic side effects would have to comprise an assessment of both sides: Both private and public institutions come with side effects that have to be analyzed. This cannot be done on a general level, but has to be done case by case. As for normative arguments, it could be shown that the analysis has to penetrate to the level of normative preconditions. On that level, convincing alternative ideas to the prior right of private property and to the concept of individual freedom as freedom to choose could be presented. Public goods policies have an impact on private spending and on an unrestricted freedom of choice. Yet, the prize is not a net loss of freedoms, but instead a gain in terms of freedom to choose goods which markets cannot provide and freedom to participate in decisions over shared living conditions.

One striking feature of the debate, however, has not yet been addressed. Actually, it is seldom made explicit, although it appears to be a fundamental premise underlying the whole set of reservations. This fundamental premise was labeled a "folk theorem" by Joseph E. Stiglitz, that is "a widely known theorem, the origins of which cannot easily be traced" and which is an integral part of the oral history. The folk theorem working beneath the surface of libertarian reservations is that "anything that the government can do, the private sector can do as well or better."[26]

Libertarians trust the powers of markets; simultaneously, they deny specific competences of the public sector. As a consequence, the unique capacities of political institutions are not taken into account. A survey of the spectrum of libertarian arguments reveals this second layer. While intrusion into the market is a general theme, the specific capacities of public institutions have not been addressed.

The analysis of libertarian reservations against public goods policies does not give a conclusive argument for a border that states should not transcend. Instead, libertarian approaches suffer from a blind spot. They do not take seriously the capacities of state agencies. Regarding public goods, two capacities of political institutions, that private institutions lack, appear to be of particular importance: *First*, political institutions can work in favor of equity standards. At present, governments are the only institutions that have the capacity and the power to guarantee equal access conditions to a range of goods such as health care, cultural goods, infrastructure, education, security, and education. Markets may enhance living conditions; but they do not automatically improve the overall situation in terms of social justice. Governments, instead, can do so in providing public goods. *Secondly*, political institutions need to represent and enact collective decisions. While markets obey market rules, governments can be held accountable for their decisions.

NOTES

1. For a discussion of the standard approach to public goods in theories on public finance *see* Joseph E. Stiglitz, *Economics of the Public Sector* (New York and London: W. W. Norton, 1986), 119–145.

2. It is, however, often overlooked that public finance is not a solid block, but usually stems from a set of different sources. *See* Stephen J. Bailey, *Strategic Public Finance* (London: Palgrave Macmillan, 2004), 131–162.

3. Where the line between autonomy and control has to be drawn depends on many factors. Institutions for domestic security need a different degree and a different quality of control than environmental goods, infrastructure, or education. The line between autonomy and control also depends on whether or not private institutions have been established as suppliers and function as autonomous institutions. It should also be noted that non-governmental actors play an important role in shaping and in providing some public goods—the

traditional commitment of the churches to education, health care and environmental goods is an example for this kind of civic heritage.

4. A standard argument of public choice theory against "big governments" is given by Gordon Tullock who says that "bureaucracies will . . . generate no public good is not dependent upon any assumption that the bureaucrats are idle or inefficient. It depends solely on the assumption that they are interested in maximizing their own returns. In the real world, bureaucrats apparently are frequently inefficient, and hence the real-world situation may be worse than in the budget-maximizing model of bureaucracy." Gordon Tullock, Arthor Seldon, and Gordon L. Brady, *Government Failure: A Primer in Public Choice* (Washington, DC: Cato Institute, 2002), 55.

5. Jagdish Bhagwati, *Free Trade Today* (Princeton and Oxford: Princeton University Press, 2002), 36.

6. Actually, a reassessment of concepts and theories of competitions has a double effect: On the one hand, a realistic picture of the market world adds to the assumption that competition is far from perfect and not a self-sustaining process within a market economy, but has to be effectively supported by a whole bunch of political means. Stiglitz summarizes this perspective when he writes: "I have argued that much mor than 'unfettered competition' is required to make markets work effectively: There must, for instance, be well-functioning financial markets, and there must be a legal framework that provides for bankruptcy and the enforceability of contracts. Among the 'other ingredients' for success is a set of laws to ensure the viability of competition." Joseph E. Stiglitz, *Whither Socialism?* (Cambridge, MA, and London, UK: MIT Press, 1994), 134. On the other hand, it becomes clear that a whole set of further factors are equally decisive for economic success as competition. Among them are not only solid background institutions that ensure systems of rights and security, but also intelligently designed systems of incentives. As for the latter see Stiglitz, *Wither Socialism?*, 139–152.

7. Many authors have recently embarked on the reform of the public health system in the United States. For reasons of not taking a partial stance in that matter, I do not wish to give any recommendation in that respect.

8. This is the title of Richard A. Epstein's classic contribution to a neo-Lockean theory of society: Richard A. Epstein, *Takings: Private Property and the Power of Eminent Domain* (Cambridge, MA, and London, UK: Harvard University Press, 1985). In using the term "takings," Epstein indicates that the enforcement of tax payments has to meet strict justificatory standards. Epstein's account does not imply that violations of this right are not justifiable, but only that strong reasons are necessary. Reliance on "the public good" is not among the reasons he envisages.

9. Property rights also play a crucial role in the Lockean version of the social contract. Ownership rights are justified through the initial right to self-ownership and through a theory of labour. It should, however, be noted that Locke starts his discussion by noting the fact that the earth "was given to mankind in common." John Locke, *Second Treatise of Government*, ed. C. B. MacPherson (Indianapolis and Cambridge: Hackett, 1980), 19. The initial scenario is not an abstract setting, but a situation in which "God has given us all things richly" (Locke, *Second Treatise,* 20) and in which "there was still enough" (Locke, *Second Treatise,* 21). So, even in its original version, the justification of property rights as prior rights depends on specified background conditions.

10. This insight has gained additional support in the debates over John Rawls, *A Theory of Justice* (Cambridge, MA: Harvard University Press, 1971). Although from the beginning designed as a theory that relies on Kantian presumptions over individuals and their capacities, in *Political Liberalism* (New York: Columbia University Press, 1996) the normative character is stressed—both regarding the initial capacities of individuals as moral capacities and the political values underlying the overlapping consensus in democratic societies. The idea that principles of justice can be derived from an initial scenario that itself does not comprise normative ideas had to be given up.

11. For a summary of the features of the "original position" and the representation of its most important features in a real political society *see* Lecture V: "Priority of Right and Ideas of the Good" in Rawls, *Political Liberalism*, 173–212.

12. From the perspective of tax politics, Murphy and Nagel define property rights as "legal conventions, defined in part by the tax system": Liam Murphy and Thomas Nagel, *The Myth of Ownership: Taxes and Justice* (Oxford and New York: Oxford University Press, 2002), 8. The reason for this view is that each right presupposes a governmental system that guarantees the rights and therefore needs the money collected by taxes.

13. Stephen Holmes and Cass R. Sunstein, *The Cost of Rights: Why Liberty Depends on Taxes* (New York and London: W. W. Norton, 2000).

14. For this distinction *see* also chapter 3, section "A Definition of Public Goods."

15. For the basic, today widely accepted ideas about the basic laws of supply and demand that have been elaborated within a neoclassical approach *see* Robert Gilpin, *Global Political Economy: Understanding the International Economic Order* (Princeton, NJ: Princeton University Press, 2001), 46–76.

16. Amartya Sen, "Markets and Freedoms," in *Rationality and Freedom* (Cambridge, MA, and London, UK: Belknap Press of Harvard University Press, 2002), 504–505. At this point, I do not question the further libertarian argument that voluntary exchange in the market sphere is itself the best

guarantee for just outcomes. For a fundamental critique of Nozick's concept of "justice in transfer" *see* Barbara Fried, "Wilt Chamberlain Revisited: Nozick's 'Justice in Transfer' and the Problem of Market-Based Distribution," *Philosophy & Public Affairs* 24, no. 3 (1995): 226–245.

17. Whereas the impact of poverty on skills and thereby indirectly also on the economy is well assessed, the impact of inequality on economic performances has still not been fully understood. For this, *see* Elhnan Helpman, *The Mystery of Economic Growth* (Cambridge, MA, and London, UK: Belknap Press of Harvard University Press, 2004), 86–110.

18. These examples are discussed in Edward Soulé, *Morality & Markets: The Ethics of Governmental Regulation* (Lanham, MD: Rowman & Littlefield, 2003).

19. The current position of welfare states as for economic indicators such as overall performance of the economy and job markets is discussed by Fritz W. Scharpf, "Economic Changes, Vulnerabilities, and Institutional Capabilities," in *Welfare and Work in the Open Economy, Vol. 1: From Vulnerability to Competitiveness*, ed. Fritz W. Scharpf and Vivien A. Schmidt (Oxford and New York: Oxford University Press, 2000), 21–124.

20. My discussion does not embark on the justified fear regarding personal freedoms when it comes to planned economies. This is a perspective that van Hayek articulates when he writes: "The authority directing all economic activity would control not merely the part of our lives which is concerned with inferior things; it would control the allocation of the limited means for all our ends. And whoever controls all economic activity controls the means for all our ends and must therefore decide which are to be satisfied and which not." F. A. Hayek, *The Road to Serfdom*, ed. Milton Friedman (Chicago: University of Chicago Press, 1994), 101.

21. Milton and Rose Friedman, *Free to Choose: A Personal Statement* (San Diego, New York, and London: Harcourt, 1990), 66.

22. Both aspects are addressed in Milton Friedman, *Capitalism and Freedom* (Chicago and London: University of Chicago Press, 2002), 13 and 26.

23. The wide reception of Amartya Sen's approach to political philosophy has had a major impact on rethinking the relationship between freedom, demands for equality that stem from ideas about social justice, and real material preconditions for realizing a good life. For the basic concepts see Amartya Sen, *Inequality Reexamined* (Oxford: Clarendon Press; Cambridge, MA: Harvard University Press, 1992).

24. For a complete list and discussion of the basic capabilities see Martha C. Nussbaum, *Women and Human Development: The Capabilities Approach* (Cambridge, UK: Cambridge University Press, 2000), 78–80. For a discussion

of the underlying concepts see also "Capabilities as Fundamental Entitlements: Sen and Social Justice," *Feminist Economics* 9, no. 2–3 (2003): 33–59.

25. In political philosophy, the underlying logic of this Kantian concept as applied to political communities has been spelled out by Jürgen Habermas: "Nobody can be free at the expense of anybody else's freedom. Because persons are individuated only by way of socialization, the freedom of on individual cannot be tied to the freedom of everyone else in a purely negative way, through reciprocal restrictions. Rather, correct restrictions are the result of a process of self-legislation conducted jointly. In an association of free and equal persons, all members must be able to understand themselves as joint authors of laws to which they feel themselves bound individually as addressees. Hence the public use of reason, legally institutionalized in the democratic process, provides the key for guaranteeing equal freedoms. Once moral principles must be embodied in the medium of coercive and positive law, the freedom of the moral person splits into the public autonomy of co-legislators and the private autonomy of addressees of the law, in such a way that they reciprocally presuppose one another. This complementary relationship between the public and the private does not refer to anything given or natural but is conceptually generated by the very structure of the legal medium." Jürgen Habermas, "'Reasonable' versus 'True,' or the Morality of Worldviews," in *The Inclusion of the Other: Studies in Political Philosophy*, ed. C. Cronin and P. De Greiff (Cambridge, MA: MIT Press, 1998), 101. Hence, far from exclusively restricting freedom in terms of freedom of choice, regulation—if backed up by a democratic process—rather offers the chance of self-determination and therefore freedom in the complex sense of autonomy.

26. Stiglitz, *Whither Socialism?*, 31 and 287, footnote 18.

9

CONCLUSION

The theory of public goods that has been presented in this volume starts off with an acknowledgment of their peculiar characteristics. Public goods are introduced as goods whose access barriers do not have selective effects and which are to some basic degree available without competition among beneficiaries. These characteristics were termed the open access condition and the basic availability condition. To call something a public good, both conditions must be met. In discussing the relationship between public goods and core values of democracies, the group of public goods could be subdivided into three subgroups. As goods that support the generation of the public, public goods are *connectivity goods*. As goods that enhance conditions of social justice, public goods are *central goods*. And as goods that strengthen civil society, public goods are called *identification goods*. The distinction of these subgroups does not mean that each good has to be assigned to one single group; it is rather likely that these groups are overlapping.

My central goal in this study was twofold. *First*, I wanted to criticize an overall negative narrative on public goods. This narrative either overstates the negative effects of public goods or—at least—results from blind spots in the assessment of these items. Particularly, it is drawn from a perspective that attributes an absolute precedence to market structures. As a critique of this approach to public goods, I have described possibilities to cope with market failures and dilemmas of collective action (chapter 3). Moreover, I have offered alternatives to associating public goods immediately with the flaws resulting from politics of regulation and from tax policies (chapter 8).

Secondly, it is the goal of this book to reintroduce public goods into the current debates in political philosophy. Therefore, I have scrutinized the links between public goods regimes and concepts of the public sphere that are central to deliberative democracy; I have discussed the links between claims for social justice and public goods; and I have discussed the intricate link between the concepts of a basic right and of political self-determination on the one hand and public goods on the other hand. The general outcome is that public goods support democracy at some critical points.

As goods whose access barriers do not exclude any person randomly, public goods serve the generation of a public sphere. Even though public goods cannot provide comprehensive conditions for a vital public forum, they provide the necessary means. Public goods also contribute to social inclusion. In particular, a principle of fairness says that the sustenance of a list of public goods is justified, provided that (a) the items are necessary means for a basically good life of each person, (b) the structure of that item as a public good is due to a societal process, and (c) the provision of that item as a public good does not result in burdens for a society that are particularly hurtful. I then turned to the political values of public goods in terms of identification goods. Even though public goods also contribute to realizing the value of promises that are expressed in terms of political rights, the more important insight is that the capacity of political communities to reinvent themselves can be expressed in terms of the engagement for public goods. Finally, I have turned to the value dimension of public goods. Instead of neglecting this side, I have argued for a differentiation of several value dimensions. As for political liberarlism, the central concern is whether or not these value commitments are compatible with the political values of equal respect to each citizen. I have argued that public goods offer this realm; moreover, they might even contribute to diversity and tolerance.[1]

The most important conclusion that can be drawn from this study is that indeed democracy needs public goods. The effects of public goods that I have described and discussed in this book are not random, but relate to the exceptional properties of public goods. This is not to say that private goods or other types of goods are not equally important for democracy. This is not my point. My point is that public goods are not only unique in that they have the potential to fulfill all the diverse functions that have been discussed; they are also unique in giving central claims a distinct shape. Public goods support the public as a realm in which equality is not only an abstract ideal but actually materializes. The underlying claim is that public deliberation needs to be rooted in real living conditions. Public goods also enhance conditions of justice in terms of social inclusion. This idea is related to the thesis that distributive justice is important, but that this is not the only central idea in terms of social justice. Moreover, public goods contribute to a self-confident citizenry.

Even though it was not my aim to give policy recommendations, two of them can be spelled out now. The *first* recommendation is to take a cautious look at recent developments in terms of "privatization." After the Second World War, a stark increase of state activity could be witnessed in Europe. In the United States, an increase in state activities was generated through the New Deal and its continuation in the Great Society Programs of the Johnson Administration.[2] Since 1980, a decisive withdrawal of governments has become apparent, both in the United States and in Europe. Even though governments are involved in some intermediary public goods, i.e., political and background institutions with public goods features, this does not mean that they are committed to bring about those public goods that have been discussed in this volume. It appears as if privatization has not come to a halt.[3] According to Bortolotti and Siniscalco, worldwide processes of privatization showed a stark increase in the 1990s which reached its peak in 1999.[4] Privatization then reached almost all sectors of industrial production and some of those goods that were discussed as public goods in this study: infrastructure, telecommunication, public services and utilities, agriculture, financial institutions and the credit sector, the manufacturing sector, the media. Even though Europe stands out, both regarding the volume and the sheer number of privatizations, it has become a world-wide phenomenon.

I am not in a position to argue that privatization is either good or bad. The important argument rather is that privatization changes patterns of inclusion and exclusion in goods. In a recent critical reassessment of processes of privatization and marketization, David Bollier compares processes of privatization with processes of "enclosure." He draws a dark picture when he states: "Today, proprietary interests are restlessly exploring new frontiers—the human genome, agricultural seedlines, the habitat of endangered species, the global atmosphere—seeking to commodify resources that have historically been regarded as the common heritage of mankind."[5] Bollier argues that these processes imply the loss of the collective goods. If Bollier was right, that would indeed be a frightening perspective. It would deprive mankind of a layer of civilized life that—according to my arguments—is crucial for democracy. Public goods are vital for experiencing equality and the freedom of self-determination.

My *second* recommendation relates to the insight that societies need public goods to develop a sense of self-determination and to reinvent themselves. In my view, there is no good alternative to forms of societal self-organization that—at least in part—centers on public goods. The second danger that lures on the horizon is the loss of diversity in terms of public goods. True, modern societies need patterns of association that differ from traditional societies. Political institutions are to some degree necessary to enforce quality standards. Yet, complete regulation and surveillance of public goods endangers creativity and civil commitment to public goods. There must be an alternative to either negligence or political standardization. What is needed are political agencies that care for public goods and simultaneously invite private associations and individuals to build public goods—goods that offer the chance to self-interpretation of communities and of political bodies.

Today, we are in the fortunate situation that political institutions as well as private institutions seem to be increasingly willing to suscribe to the ideals of social justice and stable democratic nations. To underpin these processes, public goods are necessary. Moreover, investments in environmental goods, in domestic security, in libraries, in sciences, in culture and arts, in health care, in institutions of education, and in infrastructure are investments in the political future of democracy.

NOTES

1. I should also mention what I have not delivered so far. The approach to public goods does not imply a theory of fair taxation. In my view, this would be another project. In particular, there is no general solution to closing financial gaps. Some public goods are best provided by means of public finance; others need private providers. There is a variety of different reasons for making the crucial decisions: Ideas about justice, problems of "cultures of dependency," the necessity of targeting, etc. For justice in tax payments *see* Liam Murphy and Thomas Nagel, *The Myth of Ownership: Taxes and Justice* (Oxford and New York: Oxford University Press, 2002). Another problem that could not be resolved within the frame of this study is how the very important group of environmental public goods can best be provided. Since public goods do not have to be conflated with open access regimes, overexploitation is not necessarily the most central danger to environmental goods as public goods. Nevertheless is it necessary to think about access conditions that meet standards of sustainability without expressing patterns of exclusion that are not coherent with the conditions of open access and basic availability.

2. Although the success of the Johnson administration regarding welfare programs is still controversial, the Johnson administration tried to continue the reforms that were initiated by President Roosevelt. Funds for public housing, Social Security, and a national health program were on his agenda. For this, see James T. Patterson, *Grand Expectations: The United States, 1945–1974* (New York and Oxford: Oxford University Press, 1996), 137–141.

3. "Privatization" means the transfer of ownership rights from the public to the private sector. In this rough definition I follow Bernardo Bortolotti and Domenico Siniscalco, *The Problem of Privatization: An International Analysis* (New York: Oxford University Press, 2004), 1.

4. Bortolotti and Siniscalco, *The Problem of Privatization*, 2-4.

5. David Bollier, *Silent Theft: The Private Plunder of Our Common Wealth* (New York and London: Routledge, 2002), 48.

BIBLIOGRAPHY

Ackerman, Bruce, and James S. Fishkin. *Deliberation Day*. New Haven and London: Yale University Press, 2004.

Aristotle. *The Politics*. Harmondsworth: Penguin, 1981.

Arneson, Richard J. "Equality and Equal Opportunity for Welfare." *Philosophical Studies* 56 (1989): 77–93.

Bailey, Stephen J. *Public Sector Economics: Theory, Policy and Practice*. 2nd ed. Hampshire and New York: Palgrave Macmillan, 2002.

———. *Strategic Public Finance*. London: Palgrave Macmillan, 2004.

Barrett, Scott. "Montreal versus Kyoto: International Cooperation and the Global Environment." In *Global Public Goods: International Cooperation in the 21st Century*, edited by Inge Kaul, Isabelle Grunberg, and Marc A. Stern, 192–219. New York and Oxford: Oxford University Press, 1999.

Berlin, Isaiah. "Two Concepts of Liberty." In *Liberty*, edited by Henry Hardy, 166–217. Oxford: Oxford University Press, 2002.

Benhabib, Seyla. "Models of the Public Space: Hannah Arendt, the Liberal Tradition and Jürgen Habermas." In *Habermas and the Public Sphere*, edited by Craig Calhoun, 73–98. Cambridge, MA: MIT Press, 1991.

———. *The Rights of Others: Aliens, Residents, and Citizens*. Cambridge, UK: Cambridge University Press, 2004.

Bhagwati, Jagdish. *Free Trade Today*. Princeton and Oxford: Princeton University Press, 2002.

———. *In Defense of Globalization*. New York: Oxford University Press, 2004.

Bollier, David. *Silent Theft: The Private Plunder of Our Common Wealth*. New York and London: Routledge, 2002.

Bortolotti, Bernardo, and Domenico Siniscalco. *The Challenges of Privatization: An International Analysis*. New York and Oxford: Oxford University Press, 2004.

Buchanan, James M. *Public Finance in Democratic Process: Fiscal Institutions and the Individual Choice*. Chapel Hill: University of North Carolina Press, 1967.

———. *The Demand and Supply of Public Goods*. Chicago: Chicago University Press, 1968.

———. *The Limits of Liberty. Between Anarchy and Leviathan*. Vol. 7 of the Collected Works. Indianapolis: Liberty Fund, 2000.

———, and Gordon Tullock. *The Calculus of Consent: Logical Foundations of a Constitutional Democracy*. Ann Arbor: University of Michigan Press, 1962.

Casanova, José. *Public Religions in the Modern World*. Chicago and London: University of Chicago Press, 1994.

Coase, Roland. "The Problem of Social Cost." *Journal of Law and Economics*, 3 (October 1960): 1–44.

Cohen, Gerald A. "On the Currency of Egalitarian Justice." *Ethics* 99 (1989): 906–944.

Cohen, William B. "Epilogue: The European Comparison." In *Charity, Philanthropy, and Civility in American History*, edited by Lawrence J. Friedman and Mark D. McGarvie, 385–412. Cambridge and New York: Cambridge University Press, 2003.

Cornes, Richard, and Todd Sandler. *The Theories of Externalities, Public Goods, and Club Goods*. Cambridge et al.: Cambridge University Press, 1986.

Daniels, Norman."Democratic Equality: Rawls's Complex Egalitarianism." In *The Cambridge Companion to Rawls*, edited by Samuel Freeman, 241–276. Cambridge, UK, et al.: Cambridge University Press, 2003.

De Jasay, Anthony. *Social Contract, Free Ride: A Study of the Public Goods Problem*. Oxford: Clarendon Press, 1989.

De Mesquita, Bruce Bueno, and George W. Downs. "Development and Democracy." *Foreign Affairs* 84, no. 5 (September/October 2005): 77–86.

Dewey, John. *The Public and Its Problems*. Athens: Swallow Press and Ohio University Press, 1954.

Dworkin, Ronald. "What Is Equality? Part I: Equality of Welfare." *Philosophy and Public Affairs* 10 (Summer 1981): 185–246.

———. "What Is Equality? Part II: Equality of Resources." *Philosophy and Public Affairs* 10 (Fall 1981): 283–345.

———. *Sovereign Virtue: The Theory and Practice of Equality*. Cambridge, MA, and London, UK: Harvard University Press, 2000.

Ehrenhalt, Alan. *The Lost City: Discovering the Forgotten Virtues of Community in the Chicago of the 1950s*. New York: Basic Books, 1995.
Elshtain, Jean Bethke. "The Liberal Social Contract and the Privatization of Religion." In *Religion as a Public Good: Jews and Other Americans on Religion in the Public Square*, edited by Alan Mittleman, 13–25. Lanham, MD: Rowman & Littlefield, 2003.
Epstein, Richard A. *Takings: Private Property and the Power of Eminent Domain*. Cambridge, MA, and London, UK: Harvard University Press, 1985.
———. *Bargaining with the State*. Princeton, NJ: Princeton University Press, 1993.
———. *Scepticism and Freedom: A Modern Case for Classical Liberalism*. Chicago and London: University of Chicago Press, 2003.
Fried, Barbara. "Wilt Chamberlain Revisited: Nozick's 'Justice in Transfer' and the Problem of Market-Based Distribution." *Philosophy & Public Affairs* 24, no. 3 (1995): 226–245.
Friedman, Milton. *Capitalism and Freedom*. 40th anniversary ed. with a new pref. Chicago and London: University of Chicago Press, 2002 (1962).
———, and Rose Friedman. *Free to Choose: A Personal Statement*. San Diego, New York, and London: Harcourt Brace Jovanovich, 1990.
Fukuyama, Francis. "Trust: The Social Virtues and the Creation of Prosperity." In *The Essential Civil Society Reader: The Classic Essays*, edited by Don E. Eberly, 257–266. Lanham et al.: Rowman and Littlefield, 2000.
Gewirth, Alan. *The Community of Rights*. Chicago and London: University of Chicago Press, 1996.
Gilpin, Robert. *Global Political Economy: Understanding the International Economic Order*. Princeton, NJ: Princeton University Press, 2001.
Goodin, Robert E. *Reasons for Welfare: The Political Theory of the Welfare State*. Princeton, NJ: Princeton University Press, 1988.
Gutmann, Amy, ed. *Freedom of Association*. Princeton, NJ: Princeton University Press, 1998.
———, and Dennis Thompson. *Democracy and Disagreement*. Cambridge, MA, and London, UK: Harvard University Press, 1996.
Habermas, Jürgen. *The Structural Transformation of the Public Sphere: An Inquiry into a Category of Bourgeois Society*, translation by Thomas Burger with the assistance of Frederick Lawrence. Cambridge, UK: Polity, 1989.
———. *Between Facts and Norms: Contributions to a Discourse Theory of Law and Democracy*, translation by W. Rehg. Cambridge, MA: MIT Press, 1996.
———. "'Reasonable' versus 'True', or the Morality of Worldviews." In *The Inclusion of the Other: Studies in Political Philosophy*, edited by C. Cronin and P. De Greiff, 75–101. Cambridge, MA: MIT Press, 1998.

———. "A Genealogical Analysis of the Cognitive Content of Morality." In *The Inclusion of the Other: Studies in Political Philosophy*, edited by C. Cronin and P. De Greiff, 3–46. Cambridge, MA: MIT Press, 1998.

Hardin, Garrett. "The Tragedy of the Commons." *Science* 162, no. 3859 (1968): 1243–1248.

Hayek, F. A. *The Road to Serfdom*, 50th anniversary edition with a new introduction by Milton Friedman. Chicago: University of Chicago Press, 1994.

Held, David. *Models of Democracy*. 2nd ed. Stanford, CA: Stanford University Press, 1996.

Helpman, Elhanan. *The Mystery of Economic Growth*. Cambridge, MA, and London, UK: Belknap Press of Harvard University Press, 2004.

Héritier, Adrienne, ed. *Common Goods: Reinventing European and International Governance.* Lanham, MD: Rowman & Littlefield, 2002.

Holmes, Stephen and Cass R. Sunstein. *The Cost of Rights: Why Liberty Depends on Taxes*. New York and London: W. W. Norton, 2000.

Jacobs, Jane. *The Death and Life of Great American Cities*. New York: Vintage Books, 1992.

Judt, Tony. *Ill Fares the Land*. New York: Penguin Press, 2010.

Kaufman, Jason. *For the Common Good? American Civic Life and the Golden Age of Fraternity*. Oxford and New York: Oxford University Press, 2002.

Kaul, Inge, Isabelle Grunberg, and Marc A. Stern, eds. *Global Public Goods. International Cooperation in the 21st Century*. New York and Oxford: Oxford University Press, 1999.

———, Isabelle Grunberg and Marc A. Stern. "Defining Global Public Goods." In *Global Public Goods: International Cooperation in the 21st Century*, 2–19. New York and Oxford: Oxford University Press, 1999.

Larmore, Charles. "Public Reason." In *The Cambridge Companion to Rawls*, edited by Samuel Freeman, 368–393. Cambridge, UK: Cambridge University Press, 2002.

Lindert, Peter H. *Growing Public: Social Spending and Economic Growth since the Eighteenth Century, Vol. I: The Story*. Cambridge, UK, and New York: Cambridge University Press, 2004.

Little, Ian Malcolm David. *Ethics, Economics, and Politics: Principles of Public Policy*. New York and Oxford: Oxford University Press, 2002.

Locke, John. *A Letter Concerning Toleration*. New York: Prometheus Books, 1990.

———. *Second Treatise of Government*, edited with an introduction by C. B. MacPherson. Indianapolis and Cambridge: Hackett, 1980.

MacPherson, C. B. *The Life and Times of Liberal Democracy*. Oxford and New York: Oxford University Press, 1977.

Manin, Bernard. "On Legitimacy and Political Deliberation." *Political Theory* 15, no. 3 (August 1987): 338–368.

Marty, Martin E. with Jonathan Moore. *Education, Religion, and the Common Good: Advancing a Distinctly American Conversation about Religion's Role in Our Shared Life*. San Francisco: Jossey-Bass, 2000.

Metzler, Gabriele. *Der deutsche Sozialstaat: Vom Bismarckschen Erfolgsmodell zum Pflegefall.* Stuttgart und München: Deutsche Verlags-Anstalt, 2003.

Mill, John Stuart. *On Liberty*, edited by Stefan Collin, with *The Subjection of Women*. 13th ed. Cambridge: Cambridge University Press, 2006.

Murphy, Liam and Thomas Nagel. *The Myth of Ownership: Taxes and Justice*. Oxford and New York: Oxford University Press, 2002.

Murphy, Walter F. *Constitutional Democracy: Creating and Maintaining a Just Political Order*. Baltimore: Johns Hopkins University Press, 2007.

Musgrave, Richard A. "Provision for Social Goods." In *Public Economics: An Analysis of Public Production and Consumption and Their Relations to the Private Sectors*, edited by Julius Margolis and Henri Guitton, 124–144. London et al.: Macmillan, 1969.

———. *The Theory of Public Finance: A Study in Public Economy*. New York et al.: McGraw-Hill, 1959.

Nipperdey, Thomas. *Wie das Bürgertum die Moderne fand*. Berlin: Siedler, 1988.

Nussbaum, Martha C. "Nature, Function and Capability: Aristotle on Political Distribution." *Oxford Studies in Ancient Philosophy*, suppl. vol. 1 (1988): 145–184.

———. "Aristotelian Social Democracy." In *Liberalism and the Good*, edited by R. B. Douglass, G. Mara, and H. Richardson, 203–252. New York: Routledge, 1990.

———. "Human Functioning and Social Justice: In Defense of Aristotelian Essentialism." *Political Theory* 20 (1992): 202–246.

———. *Cultivating Humanity: A Classical Defense of Reform in Liberal Education*. Cambridge, MA: Harvard University Press, 1997.

———. *Women and Human Development: The Capabilities Approach*. Cambridge, UK: Cambridge University Press, 2000.

———. "The Costs of Tragedy: Some Moral Limits of Cost-Benefit Analysis." *Journal of Legal Studies* 29, no. 2 (2000): 1005–1036.

———. "Capabilities as Fundamental Entitlements: Sen and Social Justice." *Feminist Economics* 9, no. 2–3 (2003): 33–59.

———. *Frontiers of Justice: Disability, Nationality, Species Membership*. Cambridge, MA: Harvard University Press, 2006.

Ogilvie, Robert S. *Voluntarism, Community Life, and the American Ethic*. Bloomington and Indianapolis: Indiana University Press, 2004.

Olson, Mancur. *The Logic of Collective Action: Public Goods and the Theory of Groups*. 20th ed. Cambridge, MA, and London, UK: Harvard University Press, 2002.

Ostrom, Elinor. *Governing the Commons: The Evolution of Institutions for Collective Action*. Cambridge, UK, and New York: Cambridge University Press, 1990.

———. "Property-Rights Regimes and Common Goods: A Complex Link." In *Reinventing European and International Governance*, edited by Adrienne Héritier, 29–57. Lanham, Boulder, New York, and Oxford: Rowman & Littlefield, 2002.

——— et al. "Revisiting the Commons: Local Lessons, Global Challenges." *Science* 284 (1999): 278–282.

Patterson, James T. *Grand Expectations: The United States, 1945–1974. The Oxford History of the United States*, general editor C. Vann Woodward, vol. X. New York and Oxford: Oxford University Press, 1996.

Penlosa, Enrique. "The Politics of Happiness: The Trust for Public Land." A conversation with Susan Ives. *Land & People* (Fall 2002): 1–5.

Pettit, Philip. *Republicanism: A Theory of Freedom and Government*. Oxford and New York: Oxford University Press, 1997.

Rawls, John. *A Theory of Justice*. Cambridge MA: Harvard University Press, 1971.

———. *Political Liberalism*. With a new introduction and the "Reply to Habermas." New York: Columbia University Press, 1996.

Rosenblum, Nancy L. *Membership & Morals: The Personal Uses of Pluralism in America*. Princeton, NJ: Princeton University Press, 1998.

Rousseau, Jean-Jacques. *The Social Contract,* translation and introduction by Maurice Cranston. London and New York: Penguin Books, 1968.

Samuelson, Paul A. "Pure Theory of Public Expenditure and Taxation." In *Public Economics: An Analysis of Public Production and Consumption and Their Relations to the Private Sectors*, edited by Julius Margolis and Henri Guitton, 98–123. London et al.: Macmillan, 1969.

———. "The Pure Theory of Public Expenditure." In *The Theory of Market Failure: A Critical Examination,* edited by Tyler Cowen, 29–33. Fairfax, VA: George Mason University Press, 1988.

Sandel, Michael J. *Democracy's Discontent: America in Search of a Public Philosophy*. Cambridge, MA, and London, England: Belknap Press of Harvard University Press, 1996.

Scanlon, Thomas M. "Preference and Urgency." *Journal of Philosophy* 72 (1975): 655–669.

———. *What We Owe to Each Other*. Cambridge, MA, and London, UK: Belknap Press of Harvard University Press, 1998.

Scharpf, Fritz W. "Economic Changes, Vulnerabilities, and Institutional Capabilities." In *Welfare and Work in the Open Economy, Vol. 1: From Vulnerability to Competitiveness*, edited by Fritz W. Scharpf and Vivien A. Schmidt, 21–124. Oxford and New York: Oxford University Press, 2000.

Seligman, Adam B. *The Idea of Civil Society*. Princeton, NJ: Princeton University Press, 1992.

Seldon, Arthur. "Public Choice in Britain." In *Government Failure: A Primer in Public Choice*, edited by Gordon Tullock, Arthur Seldon, and Gordon L. Brady, 143–154. Washington, DC: Cato Institute, 2002.

Sen, Amartya. *Inequality Reexamined*. Oxford: Clarendon Press, and Cambridge, MA: Harvard University Press, 1992.

———. *Development as Freedom*. New York: Knopf Borzoi Books, 1999.

———. "Markets and Freedoms." In *Rationality and Freedom*, 501–530. Cambridge, MA, and London, UK: Belknap Press of Harvard University Press, 2002.

———. "Rationality and Social Choice." In *Rationality and Freedom*, 261–299. Cambridge, MA, and London, UK: Belknap Press of Harvard University Press, 2002.

Shapiro, Ian. *The State of Democratic Theory*. Princeton and Oxford: Princeton University Press, 2003.

Smith, Adam. *An Inquiry into the Nature and Causes of the Wealth of Nations*, edited by Edwin Cannan. With a new preface by George J. Stigler. Chicago: University of Chicago Press, 1976.

Soulé, Edward. *Morality & Markets: The Ethics of Governmental Regulation*. Lanham, MD: Rowman & Littlefield, 2003.

Stiglitz, Joseph E. *Economics of the Public Sector*. 2nd ed. New York and London: W. W. Norton, 1988.

———. *Whither Socialism?* Cambridge, MA, and London, UK: MIT Press, 1994.

Sullivan, Winnifred Fallers. *The Impossibility of Religious Freedom*. Princeton and Oxford: Princeton University Press, 2005.

Sunstein, Cass R. *Designing Democracy: What Constitutions Do*. Oxford and New York: Oxford University Press, 2001.

———. *republic.com*. Third printing with a new afterword. Princeton and Oxford: Princeton University Press, 2002.

———. *Why Societies Need Dissent*. Cambridge, MA: Harvard University Press, 2003.

———. *The Second Bill of Rights: FDR's Unfinished Revolution and Why We Need It More Than Ever*. New York: Basic Books, 2004.

Taylor, Charles. *Varieties of Religion Today: William James Revisited*. Institute for Human Sciences Vienna Lecture Series. Cambridge, MA, and London, UK: Harvard University Press, 2002.

———. *Modern Social Imaginaries*. Durham and London: Duke University Press, 2004.

Testa, William A. "A City Reinvents Itself." In *Global Chicago*, edited by Charles Madigan, 35–69. Urbana and Chicago: Chicago Council on Foreign Relations University of Illinois Press, 2004.

Tullock, Gordon, Arthur Seldon, and Gordon L. Brady. *Government Failure: A Primer in Public Choice*. Washington, DC: Cato Institute, 2002.

Viroli, Maurizio. *Machiavelli*. Oxford and New York: Oxford University Press, 1998.

Walzer, Michael. *Spheres of Justice: A Defense of Pluralism and Equality*. New York: Basic Books, 1983.

Warner, Michael. *The Letters of the Republic: Publication and the Public Sphere in Eighteenth-Century America*. Cambridge, MA, and London, UK: Harvard University Press, 1990.

Warren, Mark E. *Democracy and Association*. Princeton and Oxford: Princeton University Press, 2001.

Westbrook, Robert B. *John Dewey and American Democracy*. Ithaca and London: Cornell University Press, 1991.

Wicksell, Knut. *Finanztheoretische Untersuchungen nebst Darstellung und Kritik des Steuerwesens Schwedens*. Jena: Gustaf Fischer, 1896. (Also available in: R. A. Musgrave and A. T. Peacock, eds., "A New Principle of Just Taxation." In *Classics in the Theory of Public Finance*. London: Macmillan, 1958.)

Williams, Rhys H. "Religious Social Movement in the Public Sphere. Organization, Ideology, and Activism." In *Handbook of the Sociology of Religion*, edited by Michele Dillon, 315–330. Cambridge and New York: Cambridge University Press, 2003.

Wolterstorff, Nicholas. "Why We Should Reject What Liberalism Tells Us about Speaking and Acting in Public for Religious Reasons." In *Religion and Contemporary Liberalism*, edited by Paul J. Weithman, 162–181. Notre Dame, IN: University of Notre Dame Press, 1997.

Wuthnow, Robert. *Saving America? Faith-Based Services and the Future of Civil Society*. Princeton, NJ: Princeton University Press, 2004.

Young, Iris Marion. *Inclusion and Democracy*. 2nd ed. Oxford: Oxford University Press, 2002.

INDEX

ABOUT THE AUTHOR

Angela Kallhoff is professor of ethics and applied ethics at the University of Vienna, Austria. Previously, she was a research fellow at the Center of Environmental Research in Münster, Germany, and held a position as an assistant professor at the Department of Philosophy at the University of Münster, Germany. Her main research interests include environmental ethics, political philosophy, and Aristotelian ethics. Professor Kallhoff is the author of numerous articles on ethics and political philosophy and has published book monographs on plant ethics (*Prinzipien der Pflanzenethik: Die Bewertung pflanzlichen Lebens in Biologie und Philosophie*) and on Aristotle's ethics (*Ethischer Naturalismus nach Aristoteles*). She has also edited *Martha C. Nussbaum: Ethics and Political Philosophy* and co-edited *Ethik oder die Möglichkeit einer guten Welt. Eine Kontroverse um die konkrete Ethik*.

www.ingramcontent.com/pod-product-compliance
Lightning Source LLC
LaVergne TN
LVHW080327281026
851192LV00001B/7
9780739151006